An army veteran once told me about something called "the eye of the Tiger." This was a military slogan that characterized someone wounded in battle and yet returned to the battlefield and ultimately achieved victory. This is how I would characterize Will Boggs. Will is a miracle! Being counted out after a tragic accident, family and friends prayed, believed God and, saw him raised from a deathbed. This experience has helped shape his faith as he now cries for an awakened nation. As you read this book, deep truths are going to be released. God has given Will great insight into his Word. May life-changing revelation flow into your life and rekindle your fire for God as you journey through these pages.

Pastor Ron Carpenter
Senior Pastor, *Redemption Church*

"Will is a walking testimony of God's miraculous power. Passion for God moves him forward—on good days and bad. He lives to ignite a fire in the lives of those with whom he comes in contact. If you are ready to wake up to the full possibility of God in your life, this book is for you.

Dr. Tony Colson
Lead Pastor, *ICON Church*

It is with great pleasure that I introduce you to "*The Awakening: The Thirty Day Journey to Spiritual Renewal,*" authored by our dear friend, Will Boggs. Over the span of a decade, I have had the privilege of knowing Will, and his life story alone is a testament to inspiration and encouragement. In the following pages, you will find not just a devotional, but a transformative guide that beckons you to embark on a thirty-day life-changing journey. My prayer is that everyone who embarks on this journey will gain a profound understanding of the power that flows from living each day rooted in renewal. As you delve into "*The Awakening,*" prepare to be uplifted, enlightened, and guided towards a life that emanates the radiance of Holy Spirit purpose here on earth as it is in heaven.

Steven Ward
Living Room Movement

Will Boggs is a walking testament to God's miraculous power. After surviving a near-fatal car crash severing his brain stem, this young man has been used by God to defy the odds. If that wasn't enough, he has found love, married, had a child and written a masterpiece on how we can be spiritually renewed in 30 days. This spiritual treatise is a biblically sound and practical guide to getting back on track spiritually. You can sense Will's personal relationship with this miracle-loving God that he experienced firsthand. This book will transform your life!

Pastor Stacy Spencer
Senior Pastor, *New Direction Church*

In this 30-day adventure, Will Boggs writes as one who has not only walked through, but is walking into what genuine Christianity is as defined in the Scriptures. Will has something to say that this generation needs to hear.

Will's personal testimony speaks of the miraculous hand and redemptive power of Jesus Christ that is available to all and is the same yesterday, today, and forever. As a part of the spiritual awakening now taking place around the world, Jesus is being revealed, and in many instances rediscovered because of young men like Will who are making Him known as He really is to those who are ready for what's real.

I encourage you to walk through this journey with Will and allow the truths presented to awaken who Jesus is and wants to be in your life.

Dr. David White
Senior Pastor, *The Gathering Church*

THE
AWAKENING

A 30-Day Guide to Spiritual Renewal

THE AWAKENING

A 30-Day Guide to Spiritual Renewal

Will Boggs

Published by Greatness Makers
PO Box 213067, Columbia, SC 29221

www.GreatnessMakers.com

Identifiers:
ISBN: 979-8-9899739-0-3 (paperback)
ISBN: 979-8-9899739-2-7 (hardback)
ISBN: 979-8-9899739-1-0 (ebook)

Available in paperback, hardback, and ebook

Unless otherwise indicated, all Scripture quotations are from The ESV® Bible (The Holy Bible, English Standard Version®), copyright © 2001 by Crossway, a publishing ministry of Good News Publishers. Used by permission. All rights reserved.

Any Internet addresses (websites, blogs, etc.) and telephone numbers printed in this book are offered as a resource. They are not intended in any way to be or imply an endorsement by Greatness Makers, nor does Greatness Makers vouch for the content of these sites and numbers for the life of this book.

CONTENTS

ALSO BY WILL BOGGS

Unshakeable Destiny

Foreword

THERE ARE TIMES IN our lives when we find ourselves searching—aching for answers in this ever-evolving, challenging world. "*The Awakening: A 30-Day Devotional* by my great friend Will Boggs comes to us during one such time. This 30-day devotional serves as a spiritual lifeline, realigning our perspective back to TRUTH in a world that continually bombards us with the FACTS of life.

Will has carefully distilled deep biblical truths into accessible, daily lessons, inviting us to delve deeper into our walk with God. Insights on the power of God's word, the liberty of living unshackled by the yoke of bondage, and the transformational journey towards Christ's image are just a few of the daily devotions reminding us of our higher calling—to be agents of FAITH and LOVE in a world starved of both.

I believe we stand on the precipice of a significant spiritual awakening. As individuals, communities, and nations wrestle with fear and uncertainty, I am convinced that God is calling His people to rise up to herald a new season characterized by grace, redemption, and divine love. This awakening begins within each one of us. It is the stirring of a soul deciding to follow Jesus afresh, regardless of the prevailing tides.

May this devotional be your stepping-stone towards a brighter and more purposeful spiritual life. May it reveal to you the transformative power of God's love and His word.

May it kindle within you a powerful flame—a burning desire to know God more intimately and serve Him more faithfully. May your journey of awakening truly begin today.

Bless you!
Dr. Pete Sulack
Founder of Matthew10 and Redeem Health.
www.RedeemChiropractic.com
www.Redeemhealthprotocols.com
www.RedeemEssentials.com
www.Matthew10.com

A Note to You—The Reader

I N THIS DAY IN which we live, we see society is falling apart. We see a culture that no longer has a true concept of truth, partly because God has been pushed completely out of the equation. The Godly foundation this nation has been founded on has nearly dissolved, except for a remnant of Jesus followers. While we see immense darkness covering this land, we do see glimpses of hope shining through the darkness. We have seen pockets of revival in the midst of the darkness. As we have seen in time past, revival comes in the darkest times of the church's existence. God speaks loudest in our pain and His Spirit will fall on vessels and people who have been broken through the trials and tribulations of this life. America and the world are ripe for one final awakening.

Our culture has redefined Truth and has tried to push everyone possible to accept everything. The "woke" ideology has infiltrated nearly every sphere of society and people are being pressured to conform and adapt. Those of us who refuse to bow to wokeness or this moral relativism, are labeled as hateful or infidels. Now is the time for the men and women of God who stand for truth to arise and stand boldly for the truth of God's Word.

The threat of war all over the world has caused many to sink into fear, and many people are giving up. Crime, drugs, racial conflict and rioting seem to be the new normal as people are searching for answers and trying to medicate the pain and unrest in their hearts. People are hopeless, especially as they turn on the news. The Word of God tells us that Satan is the prince and power and the father of lies. He controls the airwaves of social media, T.V., entertainment, music and is the author of confusion and creator of the lies so many are believing. He is trying to influence this generation of people to believe the lie that the answer to their problems lies in a life focused solely on improving yourself or building your own empire or kingdom, or a self-centered mindset outside the will of God. People are unfulfilled, anxious, restless, angry, and devoid of any sense of what true morality is, especially Biblical morality.

Right now, we need awakening. Right now, we need hope. America and the world need a third great awakening. America must return back to their first love if we are going to see any positive change happen. If Jesus awakened entire nations in the past, He can do it again in this nation. If revivals shook this nation a hundred years ago then, once again, God can bring hope, revival, and awakening to this nation and world. It's going to happen not only because of big meetings with loud music. Those types of awakening meetings may happen and usher in the presence of God to different areas. However, we will see awakening come when each one individually chooses to follow Jesus. Daily, we each must make the choice to follow him laying aside our selfish wants and desires and wholeheartedly surrender ourselves to following Jesus Christ. We must daily lay aside the broken issues of bondage, choose to walk in forgiveness, and live lives of holiness and surrender. We can no longer choose to live only partially for Jesus. We must completely surrender every part of who we are to Jesus, who can heal all our pain and empower us with His Holy Spirit. You and I can see one last awakening. But that last awakening will not happen until individuals all over this nation begin to themselves be individually awakened to the love of God. It can begin with you!

We look at the times we are in as a nation and the world, and it is obvious that the time of Christ's return is drawing much closer. People are running out of time to repent. If you've been waiting for the right time, now is the time and the season to return to God. Now is the time to make God your priority. Now is the time to return to Jesus. In your life, in my life, and in the lives of those in this nation and world, there is a need for awakening like never before. Today is the day to run into the arms of Jesus and be awakened to His love once again. Won't you join me on this 30-day journey as we daily seek to be awakened afresh and anew to the love of Jesus each and every day?

Introduction

AS I LAY ON a cold, hard hospital bed at Charlotte Institute of Rehabilitation, I began to wake up, and I saw my paralyzed leg and arm. I realized my physical body had been asleep in a coma for 40 days.

Ezekiel 16:16," Behold I passed by you, and I saw you lying in your blood, and I said, to you as you lay in your blood, 'live' yes, I said to you 'live!'"

The passage Ezekiel 16:6 were my first words spoken before I could say anything after waking up from a 40-day coma. My family and I had been in a near-fatal car accident when a tractor-trailer t-boned our little Isuzu Rodeo as we pulled back onto the highway from a fruit stand. I was declared a fatality at the accident scene, but the Lord awakened my body as he saw me lying on the side of the road, wallowing in my blood, and he said, "Live."

For 40 days, my family fought for my life and read the Word of God over my broken body, and Jesus, the word made flesh, looked at me as I lay lifeless in a coma, and He breathed his resurrection life back into me and said, "live."

A resurrection life miracle is what happened as my family and dear friends boldly, by faith, declared the word of God over me. The Lord Jesus awakened me from a physical coma, put a severed brain back on a brainstem, and healed a paralyzed left side. All this was because my family, by faith, believed in Jesus for a miracle, and they never gave in to the adverse reports of the doctors.

The word says in Luke 21 that people's hearts will fail them for fear. I'm so glad my parents' hearts did not fail them from fear as they listened to the terrible reports of the doctors. By faith, my parents believed God was putting a severed brain back on a brain stem and healing my broken, paralyzed body, and that is what Jesus did! He responded to the faithful declarations of my parents and family and awakened me to a new life. God awakened me and allowed the healing of my physical body because of the faith of my family reading his word over me! God continued the healing process in my physical body for the years following this as I continued to press on and never gave up on my recovery. I would post scriptures all over my bedroom, and when I wanted to give up, I would look up at Paul's words in Philippians 3 which says, "Not that I have already attained, but I press on." Passages like Hebrews 12: 1-2, "let us run this race with endurance." And I would have the motivation and courage to keep striving to push myself. God awakened me physically from a coma, and spiritually God has been awakening me daily as I have journeyed through forgiveness toward my dad, mother, sister, and the truck driver.

I had to forgive my dad for not being with us on that ill-fated trip when we were in the accident. If he had been there, we would not have been on Interstate 301, which was notorious for accidents involving semis, and he would have been driving. I had to forgive my mom for not driving and letting my inexperienced sister, who was 18 then, drive I had to forgive my sister for pulling out in front of the semi that hit us when my mom had told her to wait. I had to forgive the truck driver who motioned for my sister to pull out in front when another tractor-trailer was speeding down the highway towards us at 65 mph.

It has been a daily process as God has awakened these broken areas of my heart and I have also chosen to forgive my mom, dad, sister, and the high school friends who abandoned me. Forgiveness was my key to a life of purpose, helping me find healing and hope, and even leading to God healing more of my physical body. God has lifted me from a lifeless, hopeless situation and has awakened my heart to His love; I pray God will ignite a new hope and desire in you that he can and will awaken your heart to His love and awaken the broken areas of your life to the light of who he is. I pray the very nature and glory of Christ will shine into every room of your life and awaken you to a fresh, new encounter with His love.

SECTION ONE: WHO IS GOD

DAY 1 - HE WHO WAS, IS AND IS TO COME

Revelation 1:8
'I am the Alpha and the Omega,' says the Lord God, 'who is and who was and who is to come, the Almighty.'

John 1:1
In the beginning was the Word, and the Word was with God, and the Word was God.

Hebrews 4:3
For we who have believed do enter that rest, as He has said: "So I swore in My wrath, 'They shall not enter My rest,' although the works were finished from the foundation of the world.

Hebrews 12:1, 2
1 Therefore we also, since we are surrounded by so great a cloud of witnesses, let us lay aside every weight, and the sin which so easily ensnares us, and let us run with endurance the race that is set before us, 2 looking unto Jesus, the author and finisher of our faith, who for the joy that was set before Him endured the cross, despising the shame, and has sat down at the right hand of the throne of God.

G OD IS OUTSIDE OF our time and He existed before time began. He is an uncaused Being and an unmoved Mover who brought into reality all things. How could anything have begun if one did not initiate it. Something cannot come from nothing. For example, a Tesla did not suddenly appear or self-assemble in your driveway. Someone had to first design it and then create it. Revelation 1:8 talks about how God is the alpha and the Omega which means the beginning and the end. He always will exist. The verse in Revelation speaks of God in the present, past, and future.

He has gone before us and prepared the way of salvation through His Son, Jesus Christ. The Word *or the logos,* was in existence with God before time began and the scriptures go on to say in John 1:14 that the Word (Jesus) became flesh and dwelt among us. Isaiah 40:8 tells us, "The grass withers and the flowers fall, but the word of the Lord stands forever." The bible as we know it, is not just a historical text or a dead book written thousands of years ago. It is the living Word that was present with God and will still be all the way into eternity. Because God has always been and always will be, He is in control, and He can handle every single one of the problems facing you right this moment! Meditate on that! The Creator of the Universe has your life in His hand.

God finished "the works" required for your salvation before the creation of the world. Because God is outside of our time, He already finished everything which was required for your salvation. God's ways are above our ways, and He is not governed according to the timetable of this universe. His timing is far above our time. He has existed before our time began; this is how he already purchased our salvation and freedom. This is because He is far above our ways and our time!

In fact Hebrews 12:1, 2 tells us, "Therefore we also, since we are surrounded by so great a cloud of witnesses, let us lay aside every weight, and the sin which so easily ensnares *us,* and let us run with endurance the race that is set before us, **2** looking unto Jesus, the author and finisher of *our* faith, who for the joy that was set before Him endured the cross, despising the shame, and has sat down at the right hand of the throne of God."

Our Savior Jesus Christ already won our battles. He was crucified before the foundation of our world, and He wrote each of your stories, and finished every one of your battles. When Jesus spoke the words, "It is finished" and breathed His last breath on earth, at that moment, your victory was won if you have a relationship with Him by faith and belief. When you step into the place of the salvation that Christ offers, you step into a place of victory, purpose, and peace. This should encourage you, knowing that Christ has already won every one of your battles. You simply need to, by faith, walk into the victory that is already yours. A life of faith and obedience is key to walking into the blessings of God and into His will.

Challenge (Action Step):

Who is God to you (present)? Who was God to you (past)?

Now answer the question: Who do you think he will be to you (future)?

JOURNAL NOTES

DAY 2 – ONE TRUE GOD

John 17:3
*Now this is eternal life: that they know you,
the only true God, and Jesus Christ, whom you
have sent.*

Isaiah 46:9
*for I am God, and there is no other, I am God,
and there is none like me,*

T HERE IS ONE TRUE God and eternal life is only found
in Him. In this day and age, people think that there
are many gods. This holds the viewpoint of a polytheist.
Many think we can coexist by believing that there is not an
absolute truth found in a religion. However, that is false as
believers in the God of the Holy Bible. We believe that God
is the one true God, and there is no one like Him. Contrary

to all the other religions, Jesus Christ, who was God made flesh, is the only deity who died for the sins of humanity yet rose again from the grave. Therefore, Our God is alive and active in the lives of His children!

As John 17:3 says, when we know God and His Son Jesus, we are granted life both here on earth and in heaven to come.

The passage in Luke shows us how Jesus defeated Satan when He spoke the Word of God, which was taken from Deuteronomy where God gave Moses the 10 commandments. This was the first commandment, where God said, "You shall have no other gods before me. Many of the difficulties we have in life can simply be traced to idolatry on our part. It can even be said that we are not truly devoted to the One True God, because we are devoted to other gods.

Other gods or idols can take the form of money, fame, ego, materialism, sex, greed, sports, T.V., and the list goes on. But I think we all can write our own list of gods or idols which have choked out our love for the One True God, who created us. God has designed into the fabric of every one of His children the opportunity and potential to achieve greatness on this earth for His Kingdom. God has placed His nature inside of you, He has given you the keys to the Kingdom of God, and He has given you the opportunity to live an abundant life because of the power of the cross of Jesus Christ and His shed blood. The very nature of the Triune God abides inside of you and has given you a Kingdom assignment, but it is up to you to truly live out your Kingdom purpose on the earth.

Many people never know their true God-given identity and purpose and live out their full potential because they are trying to serve the One True God and one or more other gods or idols. God has given you the keys to an abundant life of victory, but you have to truly allow Him to be in the driver's seat of your life.

You can't try to live your life, serving God and money or something else and expect to get anywhere significant. Your allegiance must be to God and Him alone. I challenge you to examine your life and determine if you are genuinely serving God, or are you trying to serve Him, and also something or someone else? You cannot serve two different things. Your allegiance must be only to Jesus Christ. Who is your allegiance to? Repent for any way that you are not fully committed to Christ. Money is not evil, but the love of money is the root of all evil.

As 1 Timothy 6:10 tells us, many peoples' lives are in shambles because they have pursued money as their life goal, instead of chasing after God. The love of money has caused many to be pierced through with many sorrows.

Challenge (Action Step):

Meditate on Isaiah 46:9 and John 17:3 (Read and ponder these):

Isaiah 46:9 in the morning and John 17:3 in the evening and write down anything which comes to your mind.

Spend at least 10 to 15 minutes today praying and meditating on the above verses and the One True God. Ask God to show you if you do have divided loyalties and are chasing after other gods. If so, repent.

JOURNAL NOTES

DAY 3 – GOD IS LOVE

Romans 8:35-39

Who shall separate us from the love of Christ? Shall tribulation, or distress, or persecution, or famine, or nakedness, or peril, or sword? As it is written: "For Your sake we are killed all day long. We are accounted as sheep for the slaughter." Yet in all these things we are more than conquerors through Him who loved us. For I am persuaded that neither death nor life, nor angels nor principalities nor powers, nor things present nor things to come, 39 nor height nor depth, nor any other created thing, shall be able to separate us from the love of God which is in Christ Jesus our Lord.

Ephesians 3:17-19

That Christ may dwell in your hearts through faith; that you, being rooted and grounded in love, may be able to comprehend with all the saints what is the width and length and depth and height—to know the love of Christ which passes knowledge; that you may be filled with all the fullness of God.

1 John 4:9-11

He who does not love does not know God, for God is love. In this the love of God was manifested toward us, that God has sent His only begotten Son into the world, that we might live through Him. In this is love, not that we loved God, but that He loved us and sent His Son to be the propitiation for our sins. Beloved, if God so loved us, we also ought to love one another.

T HESE VERSES ABOVE HAVE come alive over the past few years. Especially after I had my two daughters, I have come to have a much deeper awareness and appreciation for these verses. The amount of love I have grown to have for my two precious daughters has shown me in a small way how much God loves us, His children. The extraordinary measure of love God has for us can never be quenched. His love for us is deeper than any well and more vast than any ocean. God's love for His children will pierce the darkest situations and break down the worst imaginable walls.

When I think of my love for my two precious daughters, I am reminded of God's love for me. Nothing would keep me from running to help or love my daughters, and nothing will keep God from running to save, heal, restore, support, or shadow us with His immense love! Think about it; God sent His Son Jesus to take our punishment on the cross so that we could live with Him.

Jesus Christ, the perfect, spotless, innocent Lamb of God, absorbed God's wrath against the sin of humanity on the cross. You try to put anything between me and my girls that would put them in danger, and no obstacle would keep me from saving my daughters! That is just a tiny picture of God's love for us. And the thing is, God's love is so much more perfect and purer than any love we can offer to anyone. The love of the Father is 100% pure and undefiled. Nothing will ever separate you from His love!

This love of God demands a response on our part. He loves us perfectly so that we will live out of love for him. He loved us so we can give His love to others (this world).

1 John 4:11 tells us that we can love others because God first loved us. The way we can love others is to love them with an *agape* love, meaning God's form of perfect love. Agape love means God loves us without expecting anything in return. Agape love is the perfect love of God that comes from His perfect character. It is His perfect love which is defined as love in the highest sense. God has agape love for His children that will never end. His agape

love is endless and there is nothing that can separate us from His perfect agape love.

In fact, as children of God, we have the nature of God inside of us. Thus, we are able to have agape love for others because He first loved us and transferred His nature to us. We can have *phileo* love for others, because His agape love is always flowing to us. There is a fullness of His love which will wipe away every hurt, pain, sorrow, and wound, and forgive every sin and defilement. There is a river always flowing from the throne of Heaven containing His agape love to fill anyone who asks and receives it.

The interesting point is that the amount of love we each may have for one another is only a small fraction of the love that God has for us. While our love will eventually fail, God's love will never fail. Nothing can ever come between us and the love of God, meaning once you and I encounter the love of God there is nothing that will ever separate us from His love. When we are in His love, that means we are in His protection, His peace, His comfort, and His healing.

When you and I are living in His love and abundance, this means we have His blessings not only in our families and relationships, but also on everything that our hands touch. With everywhere we go, people will be impacted by the love of God that we carry, for we will radiate His love. His presence will go with us, and wherever the Spirit of God goes, His love will go. His love climbs the highest mountain and pierces the darkest storm. His love is inside of you and there is nothing you can't conquer with His love in your heart.

God is love, which means every detail about His nature flows from a place of perfect love. He is holy and His love is Holy. If you and I are to live our lives reflecting His love, then our love must be Holy and set apart. Our lives must radiate His love.

1 John 4 tells us that God sent Jesus into the world to die for us so that each of His children might live through Him. God wants us to live our lives "through' His Son Jesus Christ, so that everything we do comes from a place of love for God and for His children. The more and more you and I love God, the more and more we are to love His children.

In fact, 1 John 3:10 tells us that if we love God, we have to love His children. So we can measure how much we are in love with God by how we are flowing in love in all our relationships. The more and more you and I are in love with God, the more we will have soundness and harmony in our relationships.

Challenge (Action Step):

Have you received God's love? If not, why haven't you? Has the love or lack thereof from your earthly Father hindered you from receiving the love of your heavenly Father? If so, ask God to heal your heart and choose to forgive your earthly Father so you can receive the love of your heavenly Father.

JOURNAL NOTES

DAY 4 – JESUS

John 3:16
For God so loved the world, that he gave his only Son, that whoever believes in him should not perish but have eternal life.

John 14:6
Jesus answered, 'I am the way and the truth and the life. No one comes to the Father except through me.'

Romans 5:8
But God shows his love for us in that while we were still sinners, Christ died for us.

Luke 19:10
*For the Son of Man came to seek and to save
the lost.*

G OD LOVED US SO much that He chose us before
the foundation of the world for salvation. In fact,
Hebrews tells us that the works for our redemption were
finished before the foundation of the world. Christ died
for us while we were still sinners. When we were in our
mess, habitually sinning, he sent His one and only son,
Jesus Christ, to come to earth to take on the sins of the
world, knowing that some of us would never choose to
follow him. It wasn't that we chose Christ but Christ chose
us, even before we were born. That is why we do not have
to get our lives right before coming to Christ. He accepts
us as we are.

However, we must first realize that we are lost and
in need of a Savior. The biggest misconception that
the enemy tries to deceive us into thinking, especially
in America, with our comforts and living the American
dream, is that life is great, and we do not need God.
We could drive the fanciest car, have the biggest house,
receive all of the job promotions but if we're not careful
we will presume to think that all is well.

Looking at the words of Jesus, we see that God calls
each of us to a standard of holiness, and we cannot
reach this without Christ. When Christ comes into our
heart and He becomes our Lord and Saviour, His blood

covers us and makes us holy, because our spirit becomes seated with Him in heavenly places. Jesus said the greatest commandment was to love the Lord your God with all your heart, soul, and strength, and love your neighbor as yourself. He said all the law and prophets hang on these two commandments. Everything in your life, meaning each motive, desire, thought, or action that does not line up with loving God or loving any one of His children, is considered sin and deserves condemnation. All have sinned and fallen short of the glory of God. Jesus happens to be the only person in all of history to have the answer to sin, and that is found in his blood that was shed on the cross of calvary.

Jesus is called the Great Atoner because he made amends for our sins and brought all of us who were far off to near by his blood. Society will tell you to believe in pluralism (all religions are true) and the belief that there are many ways to God, or we can all "coexist" with our different belief systems and accept each other.

But the Word of God says in John 14:6 that Jesus is "the way, the truth, and the life. No one comes to the Father except through me." The big question remains, how can we find the way, the truth, and the life?

John 3:16 tells us that one must believe in the name of Jesus. That he came into this world, lived a perfect life we never could have and died for the sins of the world, yet resurrected on the third day with all authority in his hands.

So many people wander throughout their lives aimlessly and without hope, meaning, and purpose in life. They live their lives devoid of the love and power of Jesus because they have never experienced His love and saving power. If your life is falling apart, I challenge you to cry out to Jesus and accept the free gift of His gift of salvation, who died in your place on the cross, so that you could inherit eternal life.

Challenge (Action Step):

If you would like to receive Jesus Christ in your heart, repeat after me. Dear Jesus, I am a sinner and I need a savior. I confess all of the sin that I have committed in my life. I believe that you are the one who can wash my sins away and give me eternal life. I believe that you came, lived a perfect life I never could have lived, died for my sins and resurrected on the third day with all authority in your hands. Come into my heart, change me, and make me like you. In Jesus' name Amen. If you prayed this prayer, we would love to hear about it. Email to awakenmovement7@gmail.com and say "I gave my life to Christ." Welcome to the family of God. This is the greatest day of your life!

For those who have given their life to Christ, meditate on the fact that Jesus' heart is to save the lost and ask the Father for your heart to be intertwined with his that you might desire the same.

Meditate on John 14:6 for at least 15 minutes so that each day you might seek him for the way and that you might seek for truth and you might receive the life that he wants to pour into you every day.

JOURNAL NOTES

Day 5 – The Trinity: Three People In One

Genesis 1:1,2
In the beginning, God created the heavens and the earth. The earth was without form and void, and darkness was over the face of the deep. And the Spirit of God was hovering over the face of the waters.

Genesis 1:26
Then God said, 'Let Us make man in Our image, after Our likeness.'

John 1:1-3
In the beginning was the Word, and the Word was with God, and the Word was God. He was in the beginning with God. All things were made through him, and without him was not anything made that was made.

Matthew 3:16-17
And when Jesus was baptized, immediately he went up from the water, and behold, the heavens were opened to him, and he saw the Spirit of God descending like a dove and coming to rest on him; and behold, a voice from heaven said, 'This is my beloved Son with whom I am well pleased.'

JOHN 1:1 GIVES US insight by telling us that the Word was in the beginning with God. The Word means Logos, who is Jesus Christ. The combination of John 1:1 and Genesis 1:1-3 shows us that God the Father, God the Son, and God the Holy Spirit are three distinct persons in one. All of the Trinity is sovereign.

We see more evidence found a little bit later in Genesis 1:26, where God said, "let us make man in our own image." If you look closely at the text, the word us is used which signifies plurality. Referring to the Father, Son, and Holy

Spirit all existing together and having a part in forming the first man.

In the New Testament, in Matthew 3:16-17, we read where Jesus is baptized in the Jordan River. In this passage, God the Father affirms His Son in an audible voice when He says, "This is my beloved Son in whom I am well pleased." Then the Holy Spirit of God descends on Jesus in the form of a dove. Right here, we have a picture of Father God speaking, The Son Jesus being baptized, and the Holy Spirit in the form of a dove.

At Pentecost, in Acts 2, we see the visible manifestation of the third person of the Trinity, the Holy Spirit.

In Acts 1:6, after Jesus had been resurrected, we see the disciples ask Jesus if He was going to restore the Kingdom of Israel.

Jesus tells them in Acts 1:7, "It's not for you to know the times and seasons that my Father has set by His own authority.

And Acts 1:8, "But you shall receive power when the Holy Spirit has come upon you; and you shall be witnesses to Me in Jerusalem, and in all Judea and Samaria, and to the end of the earth."

Jesus was telling them that when the Holy Spirit came at Pentecost, they would have a supernatural kingdom of the Holy Spirit to live in. The power of the Kingdom of Heaven came to earth when the Holy Spirit came at Pentecost. Because Pentecost happened, now you and I can live by the power of the Holy Spirit and have a Kingdom purpose. By the power of the Holy Spirit, we can operate and move on the earth in anointing and authority. When each of us operates in this new Kingdom of the Holy Spirit, God will be able to open the windows of Heaven and pour out His love once again. We will see one last awakening upon this nation when the Sons and Daughters of God take their place in the Kingdom of God on earth and live in His presence, fulfilling their purpose on the earth to manifest His glory.

Yes, there is a Father God who loves you and made your salvation and freedom possible through the offering of His Son Jesus. Yes, there is a Father God who provides for and cares for us. His Word is for your inspiration, guidance, nourishment, and healing.

In fact, Psalm 107:20 tells us that God sent His Word and healed you. The Word of God has already secured our healing. His Word dispels all lies.

Yes, there is His Son, Jesus, who died for each of you reading this. There is healing through His blood for every disease you may have. Through Jesus Christ, there is healing for every marriage problem you have. There is healing and breakthrough for every sin, sorrow, and shame. His blood is still as effective and powerful today to heal you of any and every problem you may have.

The Holy Spirit is how we live on the earth in our Kingdom purpose. The Holy Spirit is the presence we feel in worship. The Holy Spirit is who convicts us of sin. The Holy Spirit is who leads and guides us. The Holy Spirit is who moves upon the earth, making His Word come alive to His children, and drawing sinners to repentance.

Challenge (Action Step):

Do you recognize the influence of each of the persons of the Trinity in your life? Do you worship the Father and the Son?

Meditate on the power of the Holy Spirit in your life.

Meditate and thank God for how He made your salvation possible centuries ago by sending His Son, Jesus, to be your Savior.

Meditate on the Power of each person of the Trinity and worship God. Read the verses at the beginning of the chapter and thank God for each one.

JOURNAL NOTES

SECTION TWO: KNOWING GOD

DAY 6 – RELATIONSHIP OVER RELIGIOSITY

Acts 23:6
Now when Paul perceived that one part was Sadducees and the other Pharisees, he cried out in the council, "Brothers, I am a Pharisee, a son of Pharisees.

Mark 7:8
You leave the commandment of God and hold to the tradition of men.

Philippians 3:8
Indeed, I count everything as loss because of the surpassing worth of knowing Christ Jesus

my Lord. For his sake I have suffered the loss of
all things and count them as rubbish, in order
that I may gain Christ.

THE MERRIAM-WEBSTER DICTIONARY DEFINES religion as "a personal set or institutionalized system of religious attitudes, beliefs, and practices. There are various religions in the world today. People tend to seek religion because they feel empty, devoid of hope, and are searching for purpose, meaning, and fulfillment in life.

Growing up, many children are exposed to and adopt the belief systems and cultural practices of their parents. Even before an individual believes it themselves, he will automatically identify with his parents' belief systems.

In Acts 23:6 we see that Paul tells us that he followed in his father's footsteps of becoming a pharisee. Pharisees were a Jewish sect who followed the legal traditions of their forefathers, rather than following the words of God in the Torah.

Jesus says in Mark 7:8 that they have "left the commandment of God and held to the tradition of men." To be religious is to withhold tradition or practices that man made over what God says. Relationship is when the Lord captures your heart, opens your eyes, and out of worship to him you obey him.

A good example of this is found during Paul's transformation when he was on his way to Damascus to persecute more Christians when the light of Jesus knocked him to the ground and lifted the veil from his eyes.

In Galatians 1:18, we read that he then spent three years in the Arabian desert, where God continued changing his heart and probably revealing to him much of the revelation we now read in Paul's letters. Paul lived an impactful life for Christ in which he came to the conclusion that he counted everything as loss because of the surpassing worth of knowing Christ Jesus. He started off in a religious sect, (the Pharisees), experienced the revelation of Jesus Christ, and ended up forming a relationship with Jesus along the way. Just like Paul went from being religious into finding a relationship with the Living Savior. I have hope that you can too.

Challenge (Action Step):

Has Jesus captured your heart or are you walking through the motions, checking the box of religious duties?

JOURNAL NOTES

Day 7 – To Know Him is to Obey Him

Matthew 7:21-23

Not everyone who says to me, 'Lord, Lord,' will enter the kingdom of heaven, but the one who does the will of my Father who is in heaven. On that day many will say to me, 'Lord, Lord, did we not prophesy in your name, and cast out demons in your name, and do many mighty works in your name?' And then will I declare to them, 'I never knew you; depart from me, you workers of lawlessness.'

John 14:23-24

Jesus answered him, 'If anyone loves me, he will keep my word, and my Father will love him, and we will come to him and make our home with him. Whoever does not love me does not keep my word. And the word that you hear is not mine but the Father's who sent me.'

I know. I know. I know.

Do you know someone in your life who is always quick to say that they understand? It makes me wonder if the times that we said we understood if we indeed did. The Word of God tells us that many people will live with only a mental awareness of God but never will know Him in the deepest part of their hearts and spirits. They will have never graduated in their hearts and minds from a religious warm fuzzy feeling in their stomach to a deep conviction and inner drive to holiness, passion, and love for Jesus. To honestly know God and have a relationship of radical love for Him, one must love Him more than anything else. Our love for Jesus must trump our love for anything else.

In John 14:23-24 Jesus was answering Judas (not Iscariot) when he asked him, "Lord, how is it that you will manifest yourself to us, and not to the world." Jesus answered, "If anyone loves me, he will keep my word, and my father will love him, and we will come to him and make our home with him."

Jesus isn't talking about perfection. It's a given we will stumble, but when we do, we must get back up, turn our face toward Christ, and pursue a lifestyle of holiness. We obey Jesus and keep His Word, not out of duty but out of genuine love, hunger, and devotion to him. This inner hunger for Jesus must drive us to faith-filled action.

Anyone who truly knows Jesus will obey Him. However, so many do not honestly know Him. In Matthew 7, we read that many will be surprised when they stand before the judgment seat and realize they have never *known* Jesus. The individuals thought they had been doing the right things, but the Word of God instead says that they were lawbreakers. They were only doing the right religious things.

Jesus said in Mark 12 that the greatest commandment was to love the Lord your God with all your heart, with all your mind, and with all your strength and to love your neighbor as yourself. You can prophesy, cast out demons, and even do mighty works, but if love for Jesus is not the motive nor found in your heart, then you have not known Him because Jesus is only known through love for Him.

Challenge (Action Step):

Observe your life. Have you known Jesus based on how you have obeyed him? Does the fruit in your life match up with your claim to follow Christ?

If you have followed the Word, ask yourself if you have obeyed ALL of God's Word. Is there any area in your life where you have not kept God's Word? Write it down.

What might be keeping you from reading and truly obeying the Word of God? Is there any unconfessed sin in your life? Is there unforgiveness or bitterness you need to deal with? Who do you need to forgive, and what bitterness do you need to repent of?

Next time you read the Word, do what it says. For example, you might just so happen to read Matthew 4, which talks about the temptation of Jesus. When you become tempted, do exactly what Jesus did, confess the Word of God to the enemy. Get in the habit of reading the Word, then doing the Word. When I say "read the Word," you say "do the Word." Read the Word!! Read the Word!!

JOURNAL NOTES

DAY 8 – DWELL WITH HIM (WORD AND PRAYER)

Psalm 91:1
He who dwells in the secret place of the Most High shall abide under the shadow of the Almighty. My God in Him I will trust.

John 15:4
Abide in Me, and I in you. As the branch cannot bear fruit of itself unless it abides in the vine, neither can you, unless you abide in Me.

Psalm 119:11
I have stored up your word in my heart, that I might not sin against you.

N OW MORE THAN EVER it is essential for the children of God to be dwelling with our Father through prayer and reading His Word. It is so easy to get distracted with the news headlines, jobs that we have, or even scrolling on some social media platform. The goal of the enemy is to use distractions to lure us out of the presence of God.

"Dwell" means to abide, to sit down, to remain, and to settle. Psalm 91 tells us that when we daily dwell in the secret place or in His presence, we will live under God's covering and protection.

This covering will produce stability and, as Isaiah 32:17 tells us, when we live in His presence, abiding in righteousness, the effect will be peace, confidence, and assurance. When we abide in Him, we live in a place of peace in the midst of any storm. There is rest found in his presence and we can be still and simply be. For some of us, there is a lack of desire to want to dwell with Christ. However, like a pastor once said, "discipline yourself until it becomes a desire." When times do come when you do not want to read the Word, discipline yourself for a time when you will then desire to run to his Word.

John 15:4 tells us that when we abide or remain in Him, He (or His Word) will remain inside of us. To abide in Him means we read and meditate on His Word, and spend time in His presence through worship and prayer. His Word living inside of us is what will produce fruit in our lives.

David said, in Psalm 119:11 "I have stored up your Word in my heart, that I might not sin against you." Notice the intentionality that we see in the tone of David. He decided that he would store the Word of God in his heart. To store up means to hide or treasure up. God's Word did not become treasured in David's heart in one day. The Word became treasured and hidden in his heart after a continual process of reading, meditating on, and memorizing the scriptures. It was a continual investment of meditating upon God's Word that got him to greatness and to His purpose in life.

David's faith in God and love for His Word sustained him and strengthened his life of obedience from a shepherd boy to a mighty King. May the same be said of us. Faith in God and love for His Word will always lead you into new levels of glory and purpose.

Challenge (Action Step):

Begin with each day, finding AT LEAST 15 to 30 minutes that you devote to studying/meditating on God's Word, worshiping Him, and asking Him to speak to you. This can be in a secret place in your home or wherever you may find yourself where you just sit in His presence. If it becomes hard to sit still and control your thoughts, still discipline yourself to remain.

For it is just the flesh that is wanting to go go go. As your soul becomes used to resting, increase the time in His presence.

I personally have found that early in the morning is when I hear from God most clearly before the distractions and noise of the day have begun.

David wrote in Psalm 63, "Early will I seek you." David recognized the importance of seeking God early in the morning. We also see in Jesus that He set the example of rising early to seek His Father.

In Mark 1:35, we read, "Now in the morning, having risen a long while before daylight, He went out and departed to a solitary place, and there He prayed." We read in the Gospels that Jesus was always withdrawing to pray to His Father, many times in the morning.

JOURNAL NOTES

Day 9 – Deeper

Philippians 3:12-14
Not that I have already attained, or am already perfected, but I press on, that I may lay hold of that for which Christ Jesus has also laid hold of me. Brethren, I do not count myself to have apprehended, but one thing I do, forgetting those things which are behind and reaching forward to those things which are ahead, I press toward the goal for the prize of the upward call of God in Christ Jesus.

1 Corinthians 2:10
But God has revealed them to us through His Spirit. For the Spirit searches all things, yes, the deep things of God.

2 Corinthians 3:18
But we all, with unveiled face, beholding as in a mirror the glory of the Lord, are being transformed into the same image from glory to glory, just as by the Spirit of the Lord.

P AUL WAS A CHIEF apostle who had written 13 different Bible books and received various revelations of the Lord Jesus Christ. His resume was spectacular, yet he said in Philippians 3:12 that he had not yet attained the goal or been perfected. He viewed all of his accomplishments as "rubbish" compared to knowing Christ Jesus, His Lord. He didn't consider any of his acts worth noting but chose to forget them and pursue Christ as His goal.

I'm reminded of Paul's words in Romans 12:12, "rejoicing in hope, patient in tribulation, continuing steadfastly in prayer." When we push past discouragement, and choose joy in the midst of our suffering, and of course pray to God for strength, the Spirit of God will empower us to persevere.

Hebrews 11:1 says, "Faith is the assurance of things hoped for, the evidence of things not seen." Faith and belief in God and His promises will keep us going when everything looks hopeless, because we know God has a plan and He is using the suffering in our lives to grow us and transform us into His image.

Hope will fuel you to continue pressing, no matter how difficult life may get. When we have hope of God's promises coming to pass in our lives, we can have the strength to persevere and press on through any difficulty in life. Our hope and faith in God will empower us to press on to Christlikeness as Paul did.

God has revealed the deep things of God to us through His Spirit inside of us. The Word tells us that God has placed His Spirit inside us and provided everything we need for life and godliness. The Spirit of God, who knows all things, and possesses all the revelation of God, now lives inside you and me. The more and more we are in tune with the Spirit of God, the more and more we can know God and the deep things of God.

2 Corinthians 3:18 tells us that we are being transformed or changed into the image of Christ and transferred into new levels of glory. The glory of God will come, but first, we must go into the cocoon of life, where God molds us, shapes us, and brings us to the end of ourselves. In these difficult seasons of life, we need to let go of old mindsets, sins, or addictions.

Challenge (Action Step):

How does your perspective need to change in life so that you will see how God will turn your adversity into glory? What keeps you from having the same conviction as Paul's in Philippians 3:12? What sins or old patterns do you need to let go of that may hinder your walk with God? How do you need to change your prayer life and/or Bible study so that you may grow more in your relationship with God and understand the deeper things?

Or are you content to stay where you're at, not growing at all? Maybe God is allowing you to go through difficult times, seasons, or events to strengthen you and/or lead you into going deeper with God. What is holding you back from going deeper with Jesus? Do you recognize you are in a cocoon right now? Are your circumstances making you bitter or better?

JOURNAL NOTES

DAY 10 – "PUFFED UP" KNOWLEDGE

1 Corinthians 8:1b
We know that "We all possess knowledge." But knowledge puffs up while love builds up.

Matthew 23:27,28
Woe to you, teachers of the law and Pharisees, you hypocrites! You are like whitewashed tombs, which look beautiful on the outside but on the inside are full of the bones of the dead and everything unclean. In the same way, on the outside you appear to people as righteous but on the inside you are full of hypocrisy and wickedness.

K NOWLEDGE IS ONE OF the seven spirits of God found in Isaiah 11:2 that was mentioned to rest on Jesus. This knowledge reveals the truth and allows us to be able to make better decisions.

Furthermore, Hoseah 6:4 tells us, "My people are destroyed for the lack of knowledge, you have rejected knowledge." The Bible clearly states that knowledge can be a great thing. Too much head knowledge can puff us up and make us feel good, but in reality, deep inside, our heart is far from God, just like the Pharisees.

Matthew 23:27,28 tells us, "Woe to you, teachers of the law and Pharisees, you hypocrites! You are like whitewashed tombs, which look beautiful on the outside but on the inside are full of the bones of the dead and everything unclean. In the same way, on the outside you appear to people as righteous but on the inside you are full of hypocrisy and wickedness."

Outside, the Pharisees looked good. They had all the right knowledge and did all the right religious duties, but inside they were full of filth and decay much like a grave marked by a fancy tombstone. Many people today are the same way. Outside they look good. They even say all the right things. However, they are filled with pride and conceit. Just like the Pharisees who studied the law out of duty and were experts in following the doctrines of the Old Testament law. Some people have devoted their lives to filling their minds with "knowledge," but lack true love for Jesus, and are puffed up with pride.

I have seen this firsthand with people who have all the seminary degrees. If you're not careful, you can go to an ivy league school and even attend a top-notch seminary, and earn the best grades, but this can produce a person full only of intellect and pride, but devoid of a passion and love for Jesus.

In 1 Corinthians 13:2, we read that we can understand all knowledge, and have faith to move mountains, but if we do not have love, we are nothing. Too much knowledge without love causes one to be puffed up with pride. We can say you are filled with defilement, rather than being filled with God's love.

Challenge (Action Step):

Like the Pharisees, do you pride yourself in having all the right head knowledge about God, but lack genuine love and passion for Jesus? If you are filled with too much religious knowledge and lack genuine love for Jesus, today is the day to repent. Ask God to forgive you for living with pride. Ask God to give you humility, but still enable you to seek knowledge without becoming puffed up. Identify if you are trying to consume tons of knowledge just for the sake of accumulating knowledge, and if so, repent!

JOURNAL NOTES

SECTION THREE:
FOLLOW JESUS

DAY 11 – THE NARROW ROAD

2 Corinthians 6:17
'Come out from among them and be separate,'
says the Lord. 'Do not touch what is unclean,
And I will receive you.'

1 Peter 1:15, 16
But as He who called you is holy, you also be
holy in all your conduct because it is written,
"Be holy, for I am holy.

Matthew 7:13
Enter by the narrow gate; for wide is the gate and broad is the way that leads to destruction, and there are many who go in by it. Because narrow is the gate and difficult is the way which leads to life, and there are few who find it.

Isaiah 35:8
A highway shall be there, and a road, And it shall be called the Highway of Holiness. The unclean shall not pass over it, But it shall be for others. Whoever walks the road, although a fool, Shall not go astray.

Matthew 5:48
Therefore you shall be perfect, just as your Father in heaven is perfect.

Isaiah 1:18a
Come now, and let us reason together," Says the Lord, "Though your sins are like scarlet, They shall be as white as snow;

A FTER READING THIS VERSE in Matthew 7, we often think it's just a Sunday school verse and disregard it. Or we get uncomfortable with what it says and move on. We like our ears tickled, and this verse isn't too amusing; it seems a little harsh. We want to keep our lifestyles and even some of those sin patterns we run to for comfort. We don't like the thought that Jesus tells us that following Him can sometimes mean a life of difficulty.

Each day, you and I have a choice to make. Will we choose the way that, though difficult, leads to life and blessing, or will we choose the way which is easy and has short-lived pleasure but leads to death and destruction? Each day, you and I can choose to follow Christ or this world's course and ways. You can choose the broad way, which has short-lived temporal rewards, or the narrow way which, though difficult, has eternal rewards and pleasures with Christ forever.

If you stay on this narrow path that goes through the narrow gate, it will often mean a life devoid of the world's pleasures. To remain on this narrow path that goes through the narrow gate, you and I cannot blend in with the world. There should be a distinction between your life and that of the world.

Yes, we can be in the world, but we must not be of the world or do the same things the world does. To stay on this highway of holiness means your life will not go with the normal flow or grind of the world. You are on a higher road. If you claim to know Christ as your Savior, people should look at your life and see a clear distinction between how you act and how the world acts. You should not blend into the world but instead add flavor, virtue, and character to the mess you find yourself in.

However, as Matthew 5:13,14 tells us, we are to be salt and shine as lights in this dark world. You are to be a light in the darkness. To be salty means you must cause people to become thirsty for something more. People should look at your life as you walk the narrow road, and sense the Spirit of God inside of you, and they will want to have the Jesus you have because of the light of Christ shining from your life.

Salt also preserves. Your life should work to preserve the world in which God places you. God calls you to be the hands and feet of Christ to meet the needs of this broken world. As the Spirit of God gives you the ability, you should look for ways for Him to use you to better or add value to the world around you. This is not conforming to the world but being in the world while choosing to be separate.

God is telling you that you must be perfect on your own, but only through Christ can we meet God's level of holiness. His blood covers us, and God sees His blood instead of our sins.

The blood of Christ will atone for our sins, and when we become born-again children of God, we become justified as if we never sinned. God looks at His children and sees Christ's blood rather than our sins. A glorious exchange happens when we receive the free gift of salvation. We receive the "imputed righteousness" of Christ. This means the righteousness of God in Christ Jesus is imputed or transferred to us.

Romans 4:22-25 talks about this divine exchange. God credits to or imputes to us His righteousness. The only way we meet His standard of holiness is through accepting the shed blood of Christ, which will atone for our sins. The way we walk in holiness, is by His imputed righteousness and His Spirit living inside of us.

Isaiah 1:18 tells us that our sins will become whiter than snow. Our sins become whiter than snow because the precious blood of Christ cleanses us. God takes our filthy rags, cleanses, and makes us whole. There is no sinner too lost or a person so filthy that the blood of Christ cannot cleanse, and the Holy Spirit cannot enable us to walk on the narrow way.

Challenge (Action Step):

First of all, I want you to make sure you are on the narrow road which, though sometimes challenging, leads to life. Make sure your faith and trust is in Jesus Christ. Is He Lord of your life and have you surrendered to Him? If you don't know God yet, cry out to Him in faith, belief, and repentance.

If you are already on the narrow road and life seems to only be getting harder, hold fast, God is going to use the storms you are in for His glory in your life!

If life is challenging right now, please know that sometimes God has His children in different seasons of growth and transformation. Understand that God's goal for you is to grow you many times through difficult seasons and make you more like his Son, Jesus. Many times, that growth process is not easy.

If you've gotten off the narrow road, meditate on Romans 8 and Romans 12. What is the Holy Spirit showing you? What mindsets or sins in your life need to change so you can get back on the narrow road? Does mindset need to change to view your obstacles as opportunities to grow?

JOURNAL NOTES

DAY 12 – NOT MY WILL, BUT YOUR WILL

Matthew 16:24
Then Jesus said to His disciples, 'If anyone desires to come after Me, let him deny himself, and take up his cross, and follow Me.'

Galatians 2:20
I have been crucified with Christ; it is no longer I who live, but Christ lives in me; and the life which I now live in the flesh I live by faith in the Son of God, who loved me and gave Himself for me.

Matthew 26:39
Going a little farther, he fell with his face to the ground and prayed, 'My Father, if it is possible, may this cup be taken from me. Yet not as I will, but as you will.'

I WAS ON MY way to Florida for Spring break vacation on March 15, 2005. I wanted to know my purpose even at 15 years old. I thought my purpose could be found in speed-reading *The Purpose Driven Life* over my week-long spring break vacation. I thought my purpose was about my will and what I wanted to do in life. My will was to do something that met my own desires. So I asked my mom from the back seat of our vehicle, "Can I speed-read this book over our Spring Break vacation, instead of taking 40 days, like Rick Warren suggested." I wanted answers and I wanted them fast. Little did I know that God would change the trajectory of my life according to His will, and His purpose.

In Matthew 26:39, Jesus modeled to us what it means to deny what we truly desire so that God's plan and purpose might be accomplished through us. In this verse, we see Jesus' humanity when we acknowledge He wasn't looking forward to the immense suffering He was about to undergo, but He was willing to do it regardless, if His Father wanted Him to. In His final moments, Jesus showed us he truly felt the emotional pain of the physical pain He was about to undergo. Sometimes the plans we have mapped out for our lives are not the best plans. We may think a lucrative career is the best option, but until we surrender our plans to God and His purpose for our lives, we will never be truly satisfied. We must model Christ in doing not our will, but the will of our Father God.

Jesus said to his disciples in Matthew 16:24, that if anyone wants to follow Him, he must first deny himself before he can follow Him. It's not about what we want to do, but what our Saviour wants. Our desires must become His desires. As Jesus says in this verse, we must first deny ourselves, then take up the cross, and follow Him. *The cross was a symbol of execution. We daily crucify or put to death our flesh, wants, and desires, so that our life, with its passions and pursuits, becomes conformed to that of Christ.*

That's why Galatians 2:20 says, "For I have been crucified with Christ..." In Hebrews 4:3 we read the works were finished before the foundation of the world. Christ, who is above our time, was crucified before the creation of the world and we, His followers, were crucified with Him. Daily, just like Paul did, we must crucify or put to death our sinful habits and the bent nature of our old man. Only then can we truly walk into the life of victory and of faith which Paul talks about in the second part Galatians 2:20, when He says, "and the life which I live in the flesh, I live by faith in the Son of God, who loved me, and gave Himself for me." I love a quote by A.W. Tozer. He says, in his book "The Crucified Life," "Those who seek the deeper Christian life and those who want the riches that are in Christ Jesus the Lord seek no place, no wealth, no things, only Christ."

Challenge (Action Step):

How are your desires in line with God's desires or do you need to change your motives and passions to be those which honor Christ? Is your life goal to pursue a career which is all about you or to build your own kingdom, or is it to build the Kingdom of God and pursue Him with your life? Maybe you need to re-align your priorities with those of the Kingdom of Heaven? Write down your thoughts.

Jesus commanded us to love another but also to make disciples.

The word for Kingdom is the *basilea,* meaning the rule and reign of Christ on the earth, and the exercise of His Kingly power and dominion. We are to be ambassadors of His Kingdom, and in every area of society on the earth. God wants us to expand His Kingdom or His rule, reign, and influence in every sphere of society we find ourselves. This is your Kingdom-purpose; To build His Kingdom on the earth and manifest His light and glory in every place you find yourself.

Write down your thoughts, feelings, convictions:

Whose Kingdom are you building?

Do your actions glorify and expand God's Kingdom on earth as it is in Heaven? What needs to change?

JOURNAL NOTES

DAY 13 – ON FIRE

Matthew 6:24
No one can serve two masters; for either he will hate the one and love the other, or he will be devoted to one and despise the other. You cannot serve God and wealth.

Revelation 3:16
So because you are lukewarm, and neither hot nor cold, I will vomit you out of My mouth.

Matthew 22:37
And He said to him, 'You shall love the Lord your God with all your heart, and with all your soul, and with all your mind.'

Hebrews 12:28,29
Therefore, since we are receiving a kingdom which cannot be shaken, let us have grace, by which we may serve God acceptably with reverence and godly fear. For our God is a consuming fire.

M ANY IN THE BODY of Christ think that the ones who are supposed to be "on fire" are only the super-spiritual Christians up on the platforms, yet they fail to realize that God calls each of His children to burn with zeal and passion for Him. To burn with zeal means the Holy Spirit has lit a fire in your heart and will burn away all sin and unholiness.

For far too long the body of Christ has been asleep, dormant, and half-hearted in our commitment to Jesus. Many of us have left our first love. We have allowed materialism to creep into our lives, and the cares of this world have choked out our love for Jesus.

You have to be All In, completely sold out to Jesus. We must listen to and obey the voice of the Holy Spirit on the battlefield against the enemy in our everyday Christian walk. If a commander has a soldier trying to fight the enemy in battle, but most of the time, he is sleeping or not following orders, in the heat of the battle, he endangers his fellow soldiers and will be sent home. It doesn't work to be partially on board to follow Christ, for when one member lacks the whole body suffers. Jesus requires your entire life, not just a small portion. You can't serve God and the world. You must wholeheartedly, unashamedly follow Jesus, no matter the cost. You must serve God out of love with such a fire that you hate or detest the world and the sinful pleasures it offers.

In Matthew 22:37, Jesus says, we are to love the Lord our God with ALL our heart, with ALL our soul, with ALL our mind." This means we can't half-heartedly, or sluggishly love God. God calls you and me to radically love Him with every fiber of our being. This means every thought, every word, and every action should flow from a place of love for and intimacy with Jesus.

As Hebrews 12:28, 29 tells us, when we live in His Kingdom, and focus on His Kingdom, no matter how crazy the world gets, we won't be shaken. The consuming fire of God, or His Holy Spirit, will compel us to build His Kingdom, share the good news, and will burn away all defilement and half-heartedness. When we live our lives under the authority of His Word and by the power of His Spirit, in His Kingdom on earth, God will use us mightily. There is a life of faith-filled power, and Holy Spirit anointing when we live our lives on fire for Jesus. Will you join me in living on fire for Him?

Challenge (Action Step):

What's quenching the fire of God in your life? People, anger, lust, depression, sinful habits, fear?

Do you need to ask God to increase your passion for Him or His fire or burn away anything hindering your relationship with Him?

Do you need to study His Word more to grow in your relationship with Him?

Is there someone in your life you need to forgive or reconcile with?

Do you need to speak the truth in love to someone and release some hurt defilement in your heart which may have caused depression or brokenness?

What good works has God put in your path that you should, by faith, walk into. (Ephesians 2:10)

Ask God to fill you with His love and Holy Spirit and cleanse you of all hurt, sin, and defilement. Pray specifically, and ask the Holy Spirit to show you areas you need to change. Specifically pray prayers of repentance, forgiveness, and cleansing in the name of Jesus Christ and by the power of His blood.

Do you need to cut certain ties with people who may be hindering your relationship with God, or who are keeping you from hearing His voice? What distractions do you need to eliminate?

JOURNAL NOTES

DAY 14 – WARFARE

Ephesians 6:12
For our battle is not with flesh and blood ...
but against principalities, against rulers of
darkness.

Ephesians 6:17
Take the helmet of salvation and the sword of
the Spirit, which is the Word of God.

W E MUST REALIZE THAT our battle is not with man or woman. Our battle or the source of our frustration is not our spouse, child, parent, sibling, relative, or friend. There is a battle raging in the spirit realm. There are principalities, evil spirits, and demonic forces which oppress, confuse, torment, lead to anger, and cause many problems in peoples' lives.

The result of this spiritual battle we cannot see is expressed in sin with all its manifestations. It will cause heartache, marriage problems, rebellion, lack of love and nurture from a parent, verbal and physical abuse, hurt, anger, and even hatred. You must recognize the battle you are in. Your enemy is the kingdom of darkness. I'm not saying we can excuse all our sins, anger problems, bad days, or lust issues on evil spirits. We must stand firm on the Word of God as our defense weapon and must daily seek the face of Jesus above all else. We each have a choice to make.

Will you follow Jesus, or will you follow your sinful, fleshly desires? Will you stand by faith in His Word or will you fall for traps of the enemy by believing His lies. Read His Word and write down the promises God has made to you. Find scriptures to defeat every lie you are struggling with. Live as a Spirit-filled Son or daughter of the Most High God, above all principalities and powers.

When Paul says, take the "sword of the Spirit, which is the Word of God" in Ephesians 6:17, the actual Greek word for "Word" here is the *Rhema* word of God. This word for sword is a little different than the Logos, which is what the word refers to most often in the New Testament. Logos defines the Word made flesh, the person of Jesus Christ and God's Incarnate Person, who existed before the creation of the universe. Here, however, when referring to the Word, it means *Rhema*, or the short, powerful truths or sayings of God. So we as believers in Christ have a secret weapon to use in our battle against the enemy, the *Rhema* word of God.

In Ephesians 6:17 Paul says the *Rhema* Word of God is the "sword" of the Spirit. This word for sword is the same as the short dagger the Romans would use as a defensive weapon in battle in Biblical times. This is where we get the idea of a sword of the spirit. You, as a believer, have a powerful weapon. Similar to the beliefs of Dr. Tony Colson, I don't think we can necessarily be possessed by a demon as believers in Christ. When your life is inhabited by the Spirit of God, a demon cannot also live in your body. Evil spirits can oppress us, but it is with the Shield of Faith and the Rhema Word of God that we will stand against them. The Rhema Word of God will defeat the enemy when it is spoken in faith.

The word for "sword" of the spirit in the Ephesians 6 passage above is the word *machaira*, which was a short dagger that would be used in battle as a defense mechanism. Many times, the sword of the Spirit is pictured as a gigantic sword. However, God wants us to stand on the truths of God's Word and fight the enemy from a defensive position, using our Sword of the Spirit as a dagger, which is the Word of God. We shouldn't be looking for demons to battle around every corner. Colossians 2:15 tells us that God has already disarmed the principalities and powers, having nailed them to the cross. So every demonic stronghold that was once assigned against your life, has already been disarmed by the power of the blood of Christ. It is with the spoken Word of God that we can defeat the enemy by refusing to believe His lies. Dr. Tony Colson has said that darkness cannot dwell where light is. Darkness cannot be in a room with the lights turned on. There may be shadows, but the light bulb dispels the darkness. If you are truly a child of God, you are filled with the light and love of Christ.

As believers in Christ Jesus, we have been seated with Him in Heavenly places, far above all principality and power of darkness (Ephesians 2:6). The only authority the enemy has over your life is the authority you give Him. Demons cannot embrace you, for they have been disarmed themselves by the power of the blood of Christ. If evil spirits have been disarmed, then the only power they have is the power you give them by embracing and believing them.

Paul says in Colossians 2:9, 10 "For in Him dwells all the fullness of the Godhead bodily; and you are complete in Him, who is the head of all principality and power." As a Son or Daughter of God, you are complete in Christ, and the fullness of God also lives inside of you. Thus, principalities and powers of darkness do not have authority in our lives. This is why we are to live by faith not by sight, as Paul tells us in 2 Corinthians 5:7.

In John 15:7, Jesus says, "If you abide in me and my words abide in you, you will ask what you desire, and it shall be done for you." The Greek word for words here is also Rhema, the short, powerful sayings or words of God, which can cut like a dagger. So you can come as a believer, into whatever situation, equipped with a powerful weapon: the spoken Word of God, or Rhema Word of God. You can unlock miracles in yours and others' lives through God's powerful, spoken word. Of course, the one who speaks the Word of God should be abiding in God's Word and listening to His voice. Believers should all be abiding in Christ. We, as sons and daughters of God, can speak the powerful rhema words of God by faith into situations, relationships, problems, and people and see God perform miracles! As a man thinks, so he is. I challenge you today to commit to reading, meditating on, and speaking the word of God by faith!

Allow the Word of God to transform your mind and how you think! Use the word as the powerful double-edged sword it is. The word (Rhema) is a powerful force you can use daily to defeat the enemy and whatever spirit form he may take, whether it is depression, anger, discouragement, a demonic stronghold, loneliness, sorrow, or whatever you may be battling with or struggling with right now. By faith, declare victory through the powerful word of God over every disease, situation, hurt, or struggle right now and take your first step to seeing the victory of God!

Challenge (Action Step):

Declare These Verses in Faith: 2 Timothy 1:7, "For God has not given us a spirit of fear, but of power and of love and of a sound mind."

Ephesians 2:6, "and raised *us* up together, and made *us* sit together in the heavenly *places* in Christ Jesus,"

Proclaim, "I am seated with Christ in Heavenly places."

Psalm 91:1,2 "He who dwells in the secret place of the Most High

Shall abide under the shadow of the Almighty."

Declare, "I dwell in the secret place of the Most high."

I will say of the Lord, "*He is* my refuge and my fortress; My God, in Him I will trust."

Meditate on the following verses:

2 Corinthians 10:4-5 "For the weapons of our warfare *are* not carnal but mighty in God for pulling down strongholds, casting down arguments and every high thing that exalts itself against the knowledge of God, bringing every thought into captivity to the obedience of Christ, and being ready to punish all disobedience when your obedience is fulfilled." Ask God to help you take all thoughts into captivity that are contrary to the truth of God's Word.

Meditate on the following verse and boldly declare in faith that God is your refuge and you will not be moved.

Psalm 62:6, 7 "He only *is* my rock and my salvation; *He is* my defense; I shall not be moved.7 In God *is* my salvation and my glory; The rock of my strength, *And* my refuge, *is* in God."

Meditate on Ephesians 3:14-21 When you are rooted and grounded in the love of God, you will stand firm and won't fall during the storms or temptations of life.

JOURNAL NOTES

Day 15 – Imitating Christ

Matthew 23:11
*But he who is greatest among you shall be your
servant. And whoever exalts himself will be
humbled, and he who humbles himself will be
exalted.*

Matthew 16:24, 24
*Then Jesus said to His disciples, "If anyone
desires to come after Me, let him deny himself,
and take up his cross, and follow Me.*

Matthew 18:3
*3 and said, 'Assuredly, I say to you, unless you
are converted and become like little children,
you will by no means enter the kingdom of*

heaven. 4 Therefore whoever humbles himself
as this little child is the greatest in the kingdom
of heaven.'

Philippians 2:3-7
Let nothing be done through selfish ambition
or conceit, but in lowliness of mind let each
esteem others better than himself. 4 Let each of
you look out not only for his own interests, but
also for the interests of others. 5 Let this mind
be in you which was also in Christ Jesus, 6
who, being in the form of God, did not consider
it robbery to be equal with God, 7 but made
Himself of no reputation, taking the form of
a bondservant, and coming in the likeness of
men.

Matthew 20:28
Just as the Son of Man did not come to be
served, but to serve and give His life as a
ransom for many.

Acts 1:7
And He said to them, 'It is not for you to know

times or seasons which the Father has put in
His own authority.'

I N OUR WORLD TODAY, many think that the path to greatness is to try and exalt oneself, get the best master's degree, and seek greatness through self-promotion, achievements, or accolades. We don't recognize the times and seasons it takes to achieve true, Christ-like greatness. In Acts 1:7, the Greek Word for times is *chronos*, and the Greek word for seasons is *kairos. Chronos* is the passing of time by the passing of moments, and *kairos* is the passing of time by the passing of opportunities. There are necessary moments and opportunities that we must encounter before who God has created us to be can truly come forth. Many times those opportunities and moments are passed through serving or laying our lives down for the sake of others and for Christ.

Jesus tells us in Matthew 23:11 that the key to greatness is through serving. We must humble ourselves to achieve true greatness in God's eyes. All those who attain greatness by the world's standards may achieve a short-lived feeling of greatness. Worldly success or gain produces a worldly, short lived feeling of satisfaction.

However, this euphoric high feeling is not permanent and will soon fade when the pressure and difficulties increase in one's life. We see this truth played out in how so many Hollywood celebrities will enjoy short-lived fame and success, only to fall and lose nearly everything eventually. The principles of God's Kingdom apply to all. You cannot outsmart God. A life lived in sin will not produce a life of joy and peace.

Those who try to exalt themselves will be brought low or humbled in God's eyes. We see Christ as the example of one who had every right, authority, and ability to exalt Himself. However, He humbled Himself to a servant and became obedient to the point of death by taking up His cross. We read of this in Matthew 16:24, where Jesus commands us to take up our cross, deny ourselves and follow Him.

As Philippians 2 tells us, we should daily seek to emulate our Lord Jesus Christ. He didn't try to be number one. He came to serve and give His life as a ransom for many. A ransom is a payment in exchange for someone's freedom. Because of sin, we stood condemned and were doomed to suffering in hell. However, Jesus came and offered His life as payment in full for our sins. He stepped in and offered His perfect life as the ultimate sacrifice and the payment in full for our sin problem. Our debt is nailed to the cross.

In Matthew 18, we read that the path into greatness in God's Kingdom is to become as children. I myself have two daughters, ages five and two. It makes more sense to me how we should become as little children in our view of God. My daughters are almost absolutely dependent on mom and dad. We too, as little children, should become completely dependent on God our Father. We should look to Him as our source and look to Him to provide for every need we have.

As parents, my wife and I try to lead and guide our daughters to make the right decisions in life. Unfortunately, we have to discipline sometimes. But they will always love us regardless. They are naive and view mommy and daddy as their closest friends. My daughters are always eager to see daddy at the end of the day when I get home. They will come running to greet me as I walk through the door. My daughters are always eager to grab a hug from daddy, even if I had to discipline the previous day. We should view God the same way. Yes, God may discipline, but we as little children should be quick to run back into the arms of our loving Heavenly Father.

We should love Him with *agape* love, knowing His ultimate goal is to make us more like His Son Jesus by leading us through each stormy season. Each season we go through in life is an opportunity for God to grow, mold, and shape us. Difficulties should make us better, not bitter.

I challenge you to seek Him for wisdom in every season and storm of life and with every decision. Like a child, we can daily crawl into the arms of our Father. After or even during every difficult season, we should recognize how God brought us to or through that place to shape us, draw us closer to Himself, and provoke us to let go of something hindering our relationship. Every *kairos* season is an opportunity to allow God to grow us. (*Kairos* means season, which means the passing of time by the passing of opportunities).

Challenge (Action Step):

Do you recognize how you may live with pride every day that is hindering your walk with Jesus? God is calling you to repent.

How can you humble yourself to pursue more of Christ, and less of yourself?

How can you seek a lifestyle of self-sacrifice and/or service to others?

As a follower of Christ, examine your life and determine if you are living a life of denying yourself and taking up your cross.

Repent of all pride in Jesus' name. Pursue suffering. Don't always try to be noticed, but let God promote you.

Meditate on this personalized verse: I, (your name) have been crucified with Christ. It is no longer I who live but Christ Jesus who lives in me. I died (however long you have been following Christ) when I gave my life to Christ.

JOURNAL NOTES

SECTION FOUR: WHO AM I? (IDENTITY AND PURPOSE)

DAY 16 – IDENTITY

Ephesians 1:4
For he chose us in him before the creation of the world to be holy and blameless in His sight.

Ephesians 2:6
and raised us up together and made us sit together in the heavenly places in Christ Jesus.

Jeremiah 1:5
Before I formed you in the womb I knew you; Before you were born I sanctified you; I ordained you a prophet to the nations.

G OD, WHO IS ABOVE our time, and before our time, already had us in His mind before He created the world. For those inside the body of Christ, He chose us to live, move, and find our existence in God the Father. To be found "in Him" means we are to be living our lives in conformity to His nature. When we truly accept the free gift of salvation by faith and belief in His name, the Spirit of God will come to live inside of us. If we allow Him, the Spirit of God will lead and guide our every action, thought, and word. When His Spirit is inside of us, we will allow Him to guide us into a life of holiness and surrender. There should be a desire to live a holy life if His Spirit is inside of us. Your Spirit should be driven to choose holiness.

So many people feel as if they have no purpose or identity in life. When you know that God already created you with a mission in life before you were born, it will greatly affect your sense of identity, knowing you are a child of God. Your perspective in life should change when you realize that God desires that you expand and build His kingdom on the earth. If God defines you and your purpose, there is nothing on this earth that can change His plans for your life.

There is a battle in this day and age between who God says you are and who the world says you are. God tells you that He formed you in the womb before the creation of the world. He formed your behaviors, muscular abilities, your physical features, your mind, will, and emotions. He mapped out the genetic blueprint of your life, and even knows where you will live and the family you will be a part of. You have an identity as a Son or daughter of the Most High God, and have been called to expand the territory of His Kingdom on the earth.

As Ephesians 2:6 tells us, there is a Heavenly realm from which Jesus wants His children to live by. Jesus said in the Lord's prayer, "Your Kingdom come, your will be done, on earth as it is in heaven." Yes, there is a Heaven from which our Lord and Savior Jesus rules. This Kingdom of Heaven has come to earth that we can live in by the power of the Holy Spirit, and We live in these Heavenly places with Christ when we live by the power of His Holy Spirit.

The way we are made "holy and blameless in His sight" is through the blood of Christ cleansing us and making us whole. When the blood of Christ washes over your sins, there is no evidence of your past. Once Christ has cleansed you with His blood and sealed you with His Holy Spirit, there is nothing in heaven, hell, or on earth that can separate you from the love of God, which is in Christ Jesus. The love of God has sanctified you and made you whole through the blood of Christ. Your position in Heaven is forever secured once you truly know Him as your Father!

If the Spirit of God dwells inside of you then, positionally, you are already seated in Heaven with Him. Spiritually, we are living with Christ in the Heavens, far above all the struggles of this life. It is a matter of whether by faith we choose with our physical mind to live by faith on earth in the reality of heaven on earth. When we live by the power of the Spirit of God in the reality of heaven on earth, we will see the realities of heaven manifest on earth.

Positionally, the children of God are seated with Christ. The condition of how we feel will never change our position with Christ in the Heavens. The enemy is under our feet, and because of the blood of Christ, you and I are not condemned. The more and more we think on the principles of heaven and of the Word of God, the more and more we will live victorious over the enemy.

This is why so many people have identity confusion. They live their lives governed by the principles of the Kingdom of this world. John 8:44 tells us that Satan is the father of lies. Satan is the prince and the power of the air, and he wreaks havoc on this earth. His goal is to keep the world in chaos and keep people held in bondage, deceived and believing His lies. May you live your life in truth, not listening to the lies of the enemy. When you live your life in truth, you will know your true identity in Christ, and will not fall for the lies of the enemy.

Challenge (Action Step):

First of all, you must *Truly* know God as your Father.
Now, find a mirror and each day, recite,
"I am a Child of God, with an inheritance through Him."
"I am not defined by my past."
"I am deeply loved by my Father God."
"God has a wonderful plan for my life."
"I am more than a conqueror through Christ Jesus."
"I am the righteousness of God in Christ Jesus."
"I can do all things through Christ Jesus."

"He who began a good work in me, is going to carry it out to completion."

"I am loved and valued by God."

"Even if my parents did not properly love me, God loves me immensely with a radical, infinite love straight from Heaven."

JOURNAL NOTES

DAY 17 – INHERITANCE IN CHRIST

Ephesians 1:11
In Him also we have obtained an inheritance, being predestined according to the purpose of Him who works all things according to the counsel of His will,

Colossians 2:9,10
For in Him dwells all the fullness of the Godhead bodily; and you are complete in Him, who is the head of all principality and power.

Galatians 3:14
that the blessing of Abraham might come upon
the Gentiles in Christ Jesus, that we might
receive the promise of the Spirit through faith.

Galatians 4:1-2, 7
Now I say that the heir, as long as he is a child,
does not differ at all from a slave, though he
is master of all, but is under guardians and
stewards until the time appointed by the father.
Therefore, you are no longer a slave but a son,
and if a son, then an heir of God through Christ.

W E HAVE AN INHERITANCE straight from God the
Father. There is a deep reservoir of riches and
glory that God has for us. As Ephesians 1:11 tells us, we have
an inheritance through Christ and have been predestined
through Christ to carry out His will on the earth. In
Hebrews, we read that God finished the "works" for our
salvation ahead of time, from before the foundation of
the world. God's time is above our time, and in fact, He
is outside of our time. This is how He can have already
predestined His children and have already finished the
works required for our salvation.

It's amazing to think that we are complete in Christ.
There is nothing we lack. We are complete in Him,
meaning the very nature of God lives inside of us through

Christ Jesus. This is why Deuteronomy says that you are the head and not the tail. When the Spirit of God lives inside of you, you live with excellence and achieve greatness in life. When the nature of God lives inside of you, everything you touch should succeed so long as you are doing all things for the glory of God. Just as Colossians 2 says that Christ is "the head of all principality and power," this means that you also have authority through Him over every principality and power.

In Christ, we have an inheritance and a promise. That inheritance is that all the riches of Christ Jesus now live inside of us. We have the same Spirit of God that rose Christ from the dead. The promise is that the presence of God, or the Holy Spirit, will never leave or forsake us, but also will empower us to live this life with victory and manifest heaven on earth. The Spirit of God lives inside of us, both to comfort and strengthen us, but also to empower us to expand His Kingdom on the earth.

Because the Spirit of God lives inside of us, we should be making the world around us a better place. We should be adding value. As Matthew 5 tells us, we are the salt of the earth. We should be adding flavor and causing people to desire the Spirit of God inside of us. This is almost like the idea of renaissance.

Having an inheritance in Christ should cause people who feel worthless to have value. Having an inheritance means that the same miracle working power of God now lives inside of us. This means that the natural realm of the earth must answer and be subject to the Spirit of God inside of us.

As followers of Christ, we are to expand His Kingdom on the earth. We are to expand the rule and reign of Christ on the earth. We are to live in the Kingdom of God on the earth by faith. Faith is the key to enable you to access the inheritance of God on the earth. By faith we access the promises of God. Yes, we have eternal life in Christ after we die, but we can have the eternal, abundant life of Christ now, here on earth.

John 10:10 tells us, "The thief comes to steal, kill, and destroy, but I have come that you might have life and have it more abundantly. With the inheritance, there comes the promises of God.

Your inheritance will give you authority and anointing on the earth. Your inheritance will enable you to live a life of peace in the midst of any storm. Your inheritance means you will live a life of healing in your relationships, and even in your physical body. Faith is how you get there. Your inheritance means you are victorious over sin because the atoning blood of Christ washes over you. Your inheritance means you are seated with Christ in Heavenly places, far above all principality and power of darkness.

Challenge (Action Step):

Are you living in your inheritance by faith daily? By faith you must walk into your inheritance.

Although the children of God are the righteousness of God in Christ Jesus, to truly live in the fullness of your inheritance, you must live a life which glorifies God. Are you living a life of holiness out of love for God? Your life should be characterized by a definite pursuit of holiness and Godliness. Examine your life and ask the Holy Spirit to help you change to become more like Christ living in your inheritance.

JOURNAL NOTES

DAY 18 – POWER

Zechariah 4:6
'Not by might nor by power, but by My Spirit,'
Says the Lord of hosts.

Galatians 5:16, 17
I say then: Walk in the Spirit, and you shall not
fulfill the lust of the flesh. For the flesh lusts
against the Spirit, and the Spirit against the
flesh; and these are contrary to one another, so
that you do not do the things that you wish.

WHEN WWII BEGAN, IT seemed as if Germany and Japan, the Axis powers, would soon take over the world, and America and the rest of the free world, would come under the control of the Nazis and Communists. That is until Pearl Harbor, when Japan attacked the

American base in Hawaii, killing thousands of innocent Americans. The sleeping giant of America was awakened, and America immediately declared War on Japan and entered WWII. It was America who finished the War and defeated Communism. The World (or Allied Forces) had to have a force greater than themselves to win the war and ensure freedom for all, and that is when America stepped into the fight.

When the aggressive fighting and casualties with Japan reached a climax for America, they also had to call upon a force greater than themselves to ensure their victory over Japan. They had to use a secret weapon which they had in their possession, which was greater than any man, bullet, missile, plane, or tank to ensure their victory over Japan. That secret weapon was the atomic bomb. America dropped the atomic bomb on Hiroshima and Nagasaki and Japan immediately surrendered.

I believe our atomic bomb, as believers in Christ, is the Power of the Holy Spirit, combined with the blood of Jesus. Believers have so much potential inside them that is locked up, waiting to be released. This is why Jesus tells us, in Matthew 16:41, to "Deny ourselves, take up the cross and follow Him."

Paul says in Galatians 2:20, "I have been crucified with Christ, it is no longer I who live, but Christ lives within Me, and the life I live in the flesh, I live by faith in the Son of God who loved me and gave Himself for me."

When we truly die to ourselves, (our flesh, our desires, our sinful, selfish, nature), we allow the Person of Jesus Christ, (through the power of His Holy Spirit) to live inside and operate through us. This is called walking in faith, and in the anointing of God, or of the Holy Spirit. Too much thinking on our end or too many intellectual pursuits can quench the Holy Spirit's work in our lives. Of course, sin will and even *material gain can be a block* to walking in the power of the Holy Spirit.

The famous revivalist and evangelist Smith Wigglesworth said, "The Acts of the Apostles was written because the Apostles acted," (Bonke, Rheinhard, *Holy Spirit Revolution and Revelation*, 16). For us to walk in the power of the Holy Spirit, we must have faith-filled action, coupled with immense love for Jesus, zeal, and endurance to continue following the lead of our Savior through listening to the voice of the Holy Spirit.

In the same way, in our lives, there must be action on our part to truly walk by the power of the Holy Spirit. The Holy Spirit is our secret weapon to live a life of power, anointing, and breakthrough in our lives and in our prayers. The power of the Holy Spirit is so vitally important to live a life of victory in the Christian life and, unfortunately, many people live their lives without this power and anointing. The Holy Spirit will change everything.

Challenge (Action Step):

Are you living your life by the power of the Holy Spirit or by your own power and strength? How can you change? Do you find yourself motivated to only fulfill your own selfish desires, or do you find yourself compelled to live your life in such a way as to further the cause of Christ and build His Kingdom on the earth? The way you tap into the power of the Holy Spirit is you must completely be emptied of yourself. You must be an empty vessel who is willing to be used by God. Empty yourself of all selfish, fleshly desires and surrender to Him.

We get the power of the Holy Spirit by spending time with Jesus and meditating on His Word. There must be time when you are spending alone time with Jesus and allowing the Holy Spirit to speak to you. You must block out all distractions and focus on listening to God's voice.

Just like a power cord is ineffective until plugged into a power source, we as Christians will be ineffective until we plug into the power source, which is Jesus. I find it ironic that on a three-pronged power cord you must plug the cord into a socket with three receiving holes. These three holes can symbolize the three nails upon which Christ hung on the cross. We first must accept the blood of Christ as payment for our sin debt, which will enable us to have salvation and live our lives in the power of God, out of the overflow of His love.

JOURNAL NOTES

DAY 19 – DESTINED FOR GREATNESS

1 John 4:4
Greater is He who is in you, then he who is in the world.

2 Corinthians 3:18
But we all, with unveiled face, beholding as in a mirror the glory of the Lord, are being transformed into the same image from glory to glory, just as by the Spirit of the Lord.

Isaiah 40:31
but those who hope in the Lord will renew their strength. They will soar on wings like eagles; they will run and not grow weary, they will walk and not be faint.

T HERE IS GREATNESS INSIDE you which is waiting to be revealed. What will it take for the greatness inside of you to be revealed? There is a glory God wants you to walk into (2 Corinthians 3:18). Christ has placed part of his nature in person inside of you. When you put your faith in Christ for salvation, and the grace of God redeemed you, you were transferred from a place of spiritual poverty to being spiritually rich in the blessings of God. You stepped into greatness. Your entire life has a process of you discovering the real person God created you to become.

Just like how I was in a physical coma, each of us must be awakened from the spiritual coma we were in before Christ. The more and more we each step into the love of Jesus and experience his grace, the more we understand who God has called us to be, and the more we know and comprehend the fullness of God's love. God is called greatness, but just like a baby or toddler can't do all it has the potential to do, you and I have to go through the storms of life before we are at our full potential.

In the coma 17 years ago, God already knew who I would become and how I would recover, but I would have to go through a process before I arrived there. I first had to be awakened and re-learn how to do everything. Each Christ follower must be awakened to the love of God, and we must learn an entirely new way of life. God has our whole life story written, which includes our purpose, but we can't walk it out on day one. There is a process each of us must go through to be ready for all God has planned for us. 1 Peter 1:3 says, **3** Blessed *be* the God and Father of our Lord Jesus Christ, who according to His abundant mercy has begotten us again to a living hope through the resurrection of Jesus Christ from the dead." We are born into the living hope of Jesus Christ and our inheritance in Him. It is later in our Christian walks that as 1 Peter 1:6 tells us, "if need be you have been grieved by various trials, verse 7, "That the genuineness of your faith, being much more precious than gold that perishes, may be found to praise, honor, and glory..." We are born again into God's kingdom. However, later, it is the fires and trials of life that God brings us through so that the genuineness of our faith can be revealed.

Like an oak tree, which hazards the storms of life and stands alone, we are not at our true potential until we have weathered the storms of life and we can say, "Having done all, I stand." Sometimes we stand alone. The way we will stand is for our roots to run down deep into Christ, much like an oak tree's roots will give it a solid foundation.

Eagles fly alone. But what does the Bible say about Eagles, "those who wait on the Lord shall renew their strength. They shall mount up with wings like Eagles; they shall run and not grow weary; they shall walk and not faint."

Eagles fly alone, but it is the eagle in God's Kingdom to whom he gives remarkable strength, and upholds by His mighty right hand. Though you may fly alone when you wait on God and trust in him, he will renew your strength, and you shall mount up with wings and soar like an eagle. In the waiting process is where we gain strength to walk into the greatness God has for us.

Yes, God wants you to achieve greatness. One way to do this in life is to be rooted in God's love so we can stand firm during the trials of life. You and I must be rooted in God's love through prayer, worship, and Bible study. Another way we can achieve greatness is by realizing the power of the Spirit of God inside of us.

1 John 4:4 says, "Greater is He who is in you than He who is in the world." As a believer in Christ, you must realize that there is great potential inside of you, because the Spirit of God lives inside of you. The same spirit of Christ who rose from the grave abides inside of you. This should create a sense of destiny and victory inside of you. Whatever storm you are in right now, you are able to overcome because of the Spirit of God living inside of you. Nothing you are facing catches God by surprise. You can overcome every battle you face. Through Christ's death on the cross, you've already won every battle.

Challenge (Action Step):

Are you really living in greatness or are you simply going through the motions or merely surviving? Are you believing lies about yourself, and if so, how can you replace those lies with the truth of God's Word? What needs to change in your life? What new patterns do you need to develop or what sins or habits do you need to let go of that might be keeping you from greatness? How can you tap into the greatness God has for you? Daily posture yourself to receive all God has for you. Ask God to show you what is holding you back? You should have a morning time of prayer, or possibly evening (morning is usually best). Pray and ask the Holy Spirit to fill your heart with His love and cleanse you from any defilement which may be hindering the flow of His love to your heart.

Seek out a prayer partner to pray with you about what might be causing you to not live in God's greatness.

Pray and ask God to show you if you are isolating yourself. Proverbs tells us "A man who isolates himself, seeks his own desire." You can't accomplish the plans God has for you and achieve the greatness you were born for if you are isolating yourself and forsaking community, namely the body of Christ.

Seek out healthy, Christ-centered relationships and look for ways to be a part of the body of Christ so you can achieve your true greatness in His Kingdom.

JOURNAL NOTES

DAY 20 – PURPOSE

Psalm 139:13-18

For You formed my inward parts; You covered me in my mother's womb. I will praise You, for I am fearfully and wonderfully made; Marvelous are Your works, And that my soul knows very well. My frame was not hidden from You, When I was made in secret, And skillfully wrought in the lowest parts of the earth. Your eyes saw my substance, being yet unformed. And in Your book they all were written, The days fashioned for me, When as yet there were none of them. How precious also are Your thoughts to me, O God! How great is the sum of them! If I should count them, they would be more in number than the sand; When I awake, I am still with You.

MANY MESSAGES COME TO us daily, from social media platforms, news outlets, music, cartoons, and movies. Truth is no longer defined absolutely. Rather the culture and our world are feeding us the lie that there is only something called relative truth. This means that we can do whatever feels good to us, and the consequences don't matter. This is mainly due to the fact of the message that we have evolved over billions of years and there is no such thing as a God who created us and has a plan and purpose for our lives.

From this viewpoint, our purpose in life is simply to exist and enjoy the American dream or our best life now. Many people feel that since there is no God who created them, then they have no true purpose or meaning in life, but they are destined only to try to enjoy life and then die to be eaten by worms, with no hope of an afterlife with God our Father and creator.

We must understand that Almighty God formed us and made us! He is our architect, and He has created us to expand His Kingdom on the earth. Jeremiah 1:5 tells us that God has already called us and ordained us. He has already "known" us and orchestrated every detail of our lives, including the vocation we choose. He already has laid out the plans of our lives. This should give you a sense of enlightenment, knowing God has called you and ordained you for a purpose of making His name famous on the earth. As a child of God, you have not been destined and created to live your life solely for yourself. You have been called and created to live your life out of love for Jesus by being the hands and feet of Jesus to a broken world.

We see in our society a syncretism where people try to blend in truth with the world. Our world is so steeped in sin and brokenness that everything people are doing is trying to blend in darkness with a little bit of the Christian values and say it's okay. You cannot be living in the world, trying to live out the assignment God has for your life, while at the same time trying to build a kingdom in this world and adopting the principles of this world. Your assignment is to build the Kingdom of God and manifest His glory through whatever vocation you choose.

There must be a distinct difference in how you live your life and how the world operates. There is nothing wrong with making money, but that should not be your only focus. Your focus should be to manifest the glory of God and spread the love of Christ to all those you come into contact with and, if you make money, it should be funneled into this principle of building God's Kingdom on earth.

The word Kingdom in the Bible is translated as *Basilea.* This means the rule and reign of God on the earth and the exercise of His Kingly power and domain. Romans 14:17 tells us the Kingdom of God is righteousness, love, joy, and peace in the Holy Spirit. So the way you can further His Kingdom on the earth is to live your life in such a way that the Great Commission is fulfilled, and the Gospel of Jesus Christ is proclaimed and disciples are made. But, also, you must strive to live your life so that every action you take is guided by the Holy Spirit in righteousness, love, joy, and peace.

It is amazing how Psalm 139 tells us that "God sees our substance" before we are born. This means you have potential and greatness inside of you! You're not a randomly formed cluster of cells. You're an intelligent person designed by God Himself. He knows the fabric of our lives. God has placed you on this earth to manifest His love to others and He knows exactly how you are formed and, in fact, He created you with everything you need to fulfill your life's purpose. You're a masterpiece. Go and allow yourself to be used by God to change this world.

Challenge (Action Step)

I challenge you to ask yourself if your desire in life is to manifest and build the Kingdom of God or your own Kingdom. How do you need to reorient your priorities? Pray and ask the Holy Spirit to show you what needs to change for you to live your life in such a way as to only further God's Kingdom. Repent of all selfish pride and/or greediness. Ask God for clarity of your purpose and seek His face above all else. When you seek His face, He will reveal your next steps. Proverbs 3:5-6 tells us, "Trust in the Lord with all your heart and lean not on your own understanding. In all your ways acknowledge Him and He will direct your paths.

JOURNAL NOTES

SECTION FIVE: BUILT DIFFERENT (HOLINESS)

DAY 21 – MONEY, FAME, AND POPULARITY

James 4:10
Humble yourselves under the mighty hand of God that He may exalt you in due time.

Matthew 16:26
For what profit is it to a man if he gains the whole world, and loses his own soul? Or what will a man give in exchange for his soul?

1 Timothy 6:10
For the love of money is a root of all kinds of evil, for which some have strayed from the faith in their greediness and pierced themselves through with many sorrows.

James 5:1-3
Come now, you rich, weep and howl for your miseries that are coming upon you! **2** *Your riches are corrupted, and your garments are moth-eaten.* **3** *Your gold and silver are corroded, and their corrosion will be a witness against you and will eat your flesh like fire. You have heaped up treasure in the last days.*

O UR WORLD HAS IT backwards. Culture and society try to tell you that the main goal for your life should be to make the big money, money, money. So many of us make material gain the focus of our lives and the lives of our families. Parents try to get their children into the best colleges so that one day they will have the opportunity to make the most money. The love of money is what drives us to work extremely hard so that one day we can drive the fancy car and have the nice house and all the fun, fancy things we think about when we think about the American dream. We become so focused on pursuing our own personal gain that we lose sight of our Christian faith.

As we read in 1 Timothy 6:10, we read that the love of money will cause one to be pierced through with many sorrows. The love of money is the root of all kinds of evil. In this passage, we see that it is the "love" of money that will lead to all kinds of evil. When you and I love or worship money as if it is an idol, to where it comes between us and our love for God, then this is where danger comes. Our sole focus in life should be to worship God by our actions, not worship money.

Take Judas, for example. He was the disciple whom Jesus put in charge of the money bag. When he was in charge of the money, he would keep some back for himself. However, this love of money grew to the point that it led him to betray Jesus and sell him to be crucified for a bag of silver coins. Our love of money will not only affect us, but it can also lead to the downfall of those around us.

Your focus should not be only on material gain, but on laying up treasures in Heaven. As we see in James 5, so many people have been focused on storing up "treasures" on earth in the last days. All those "treasures" are only going to ruin and rot away over time. The fancy car you buy immediately drops thousands of dollars in value the moment you drive it off the car lot. Those nice rims will start rusting, too, if you don't clean them. The CD in your new vehicle will eventually break, and your seats will get stains on them. The material possessions of this life wear out and ruin, no matter how much money we spend on them initially. This world is slowly dissolving as well as all the material possessions and vain pursuits in it. Even in America, we see the almighty dollar, which we never thought could be affected, quickly losing value because of massive inflation. Nothing in this life lasts.

We look at Hollywood and/or see all the big figures up on stage and think they have it all together. We want what they have. We desire fame and recognition. We want the big name and the big stage and popularity with celebrity status. However, what most people don't realize is that most of the people on T.V. or on the platforms have the same problems normal people have. Many times, the ones in Hollywood have lives which are miserable. You can see how many Hollywood marriages last only a few months and end in divorce.

The message of the Matthew 16 passage should be spoken of here. Just like many of the Hollywood figures, you can have all the riches and fame the world offers, but if you don't have Christ you will lose your own soul. The riches and fame are fun for a season, but that is just it. The pleasure you get from them only lasts for a season. The glory from riches and fame is very short-lived. Only Jesus satisfies.

Many of you reading this need a paradigm shift. As James 4 tells us, we should first humble ourselves, and then God will exalt and lift us up in due time. The world wants you to try to get ahead and promote yourself. The world wants you to live "your best life now" and focus on getting ahead in life. The concept of humbling yourself is unheard of. Everyone wants fame and fortune. But they don't want to do the right things to get there. God says He will exalt us "in due time." Nobody wants to wait for "due time." God wants to first develop your character and develop discipline and humility in you. If you try to promote yourself, you will end up in failure every time. Only when we let God promote us will the end result be worthwhile and lasting.

Challenge (Action Step):

Make sure you are paying back into the Kingdom of God through tithing. God asks for at least 10%. This shows that money does not have control of your heart, but God does. Repent for any love of money or material gain. Ask God to cleanse your heart of all defilement and sin.

If you have a desire to be known or have fame, it is most likely because your love of God has dwindled. You probably have an unmet need for affirmation and attention from the past that only God can meet. Only God can heal your heart.

Spend some time asking God to heal the pain in your heart from that unmet need. Choose to forgive one or both parents for not meeting that need. Ask the love of Jesus to fill your heart and heal all pain and defilement.

JOURNAL NOTES

DAY 22 – PRIDE

Proverbs 8:18
The fear of the Lord is to hate evil; Pride and arrogance and the evil way.

P RIDE IS ONE OF the oldest sins there is. Pride is what got Satan kicked out of heaven. Pride will feel good at first, but it can lead to your downfall and ultimate humiliation. James 4:10 tells us, "God resists (or opposes) the proud, but gives grace to the humble." The Greek word for opposes can be compared to "rages war against." Having pride and feeling the happy feeling brings short-lived fulfillment, but short-lived is exactly what will happen with those feelings. They will not last long but will quickly fade.

Pride is what got Adam and Eve kicked out of the Garden of Eden. They bought into the lie that eating of the fruit of the knowledge of good and evil would make them equal with God.

We look at David in how he became prideful about the size of Israel and called for a census to be called of all Israel. He wanted to number Israel for his own sake to see how great the kingdom of Israel had become. This led to God's judgment on David and on Israel. When we allow pride to fill our hearts, it will result in a penalty, and it can affect the lives of those around us. We look at so many examples of present-day figures or even those people from the recent past, and we can see that so many times when a minister or public figure gets a big name and gets under the spotlight, the pride will soon lead to a fall, and it can negatively affect those around us.

So with whatever place in life you find yourself, remember don't be prideful. Don't try to get that place in the spotlight, because you want to be noticed or you want the attention. It may feel good at the time, but the end result can be a little painful. It will also cause those closest to you and around you to feel some of the aftermath. Those closest to you will feel the turmoil and difficulty.

Challenge (Action Step):

Heart check: The things that you have done for God, or at least you thought you were doing for God, check the motive of your heart and see why you did them? Was it for the glory of God or done out of love for His children? Was it for your own glory so that you could be noticed or gain some type of recognition? Are there any selfish motives in how you serve others or how you try to serve God?

Consider Philippians 2:3-5 "*Let* nothing *be done* through selfish ambition or conceit, but in lowliness of mind let each esteem others better than himself. Let each of you look out not only for his own interests, but also for the interests of others."

If you have checked your heart and it seems evident that you have made your own self god by living life the way you want to and putting yourself before others. Confess to God of your pride or selfish ambition, ask for His forgiveness, turn aside from your evil ways and look to Jesus. Choose to walk in humility.

Each day, start your mornings on your knees before Jesus in worship. It is impossible to look at the king of kings while at the same time exalting yourself. When you look at Jesus you see how awesome He is and how imperfect you are.

JOURNAL NOTES

Day 23 – Instant Gratification

Hebrews 10:36
For you have need of endurance, so that after you have done the will of God, you may receive the promise.

Genesis 25:29-34
Now Jacob cooked a stew; and Esau came in from the field, and he was weary. And Esau said to Jacob, "Please feed me with that same red stew, for I am weary." Therefore his name was called Edom. But Jacob said, "Sell me your birthright as of this day." And Esau said, "Look, I am about to die; so what is this birthright to me?" Then Jacob said, "Swear to

me as of this day." So he swore to him, and sold his birthright to Jacob. And Jacob gave Esau bread and stew of lentils; then he ate and drank, arose, and went his way. Thus Esau despised his birthright.

Galatians 6:9
And let us not grow weary while doing good, for in due season we shall reap if we do not lose heart.

T HE WORLDLY CULTURE IS used to having instant access, everything being super fast-paced, answers with the click of a mouse, and having success with no strings attached. We're used to drive-thru's, Amazon two day shipping, high speed internet, certifications that require only three months to earn, and answers to all of life's problems found with the click of a mouse on Google. We see a generation who feels entitled to have everything at the tips of their fingers and have answers within milliseconds.

We see a generation of people who are impatient and, particularly in the body of Christ, don't understand the concept of persevering in Godliness through the difficult times.

For example, in the past when I began college I would sign up for a class, but then when it got difficult or challenging for me, I would withdraw. I didn't want to put in the difficult work of enduring to the end and receiving the prize of a passing or non-passing grade.

However, I have adopted the habit of persevering to the end. Typically, when a professor sees a student is persevering with the challenging course load, he will give a little extra help. This is a picture of God's version of faithful endurance. So many get into their Christian lives, and too early give up and throw in the towel.

Galatians 6:9 tells us "Do not grow weary in doing good, for in due season you will reap if you do not lose heart." Every difficult season of your life will always lead to another season of breakthrough and victory. However, if you lose heart and quit early on, you will never know the joy of finishing well and receiving the promise. If it's not a season of reaping the rewards of your labor right now, then just hold on, for you're about to walk into a season of harvest.

I am an avid cross-country, long-distance runner. I love disciplining my body and pushing it to the limits on long distance ultra-marathon races. No matter how tired I am or how much my body hurts, I always find the courage and strength to continue pushing myself to run towards the finish line. Even if I fall repeatedly, I will always get back up and continue running even if I am covered in blood.

By "patient endurance" God wants us to run the race of life (Hebrews 10:36). God's intention for you is to never give up or stop in your faith journey no matter how challenging life becomes. We must learn the spiritual discipline of enduring to the end, in every season of life.

Take Jacob and Esau for example. Esau gave up his birthright for one bowl of soup, because he gave in to the longing to satisfy his fleshly appetite instantly. If he had only endured a few moments more, he would have saved his birthright. Though God turned His situation out for good, because Christ came through the lineage of Jacob. But the point still stands. Essau gave up too soon, and paid the price, for he lost his birthright, that which was most valuable to Him. God is calling each of us to endure in Godliness in every situation of our lives, and He will sustain us, empower us, and reward us in the end, if we do not lose heart.

Challenge (Action Step):

Work on training your mind to finish tasks or projects that you have begun. Train yourself to quit the habit of quitting jobs prematurely.

Ask God to give you patient endurance to finish the assignments in your life that He has given you to do. Practice self-discipline and strive to live a Holy life. Focus your life on Christ and living for Him. For one week, strive to abstain from something you have been relying on other than Christ. Let one or more sins, habits, distractions, or addictions in your life die, so that Christ may have more influence and authority in your life. Once you have mastered that, increase to two and three weeks.

Galatians 2:20, "For I am crucified with Christ. It is no longer I who live and the life which I live in the flesh, I live by faith in the Son of God, who loved me and gave Himself for me." Pursue holiness. Re-orient your life so that Christ Jesus is magnified through your every thought, action, word, and deed. Live not through your own strength, but through Christ and His strength.

JOURNAL NOTES

DAY 24 – TRUE FREEDOM

Galatians 5:13
For you, brethren, have been called to liberty; only do not use liberty as an opportunity for the flesh, but through love serve one another.

John 8:36
Therefore, if the Son makes you free, you shall be free indeed.

Romans 6:1,2
What shall we say then? Shall we continue in sin that grace may abound? Certainly not! How shall we who died to sin live any longer in it?

I N OUR WORLD, FREEDOM is defined in different ways. In the context of government, or in a legal sense, Americans view freedom as being citizens of the United States of America with all the basic rights of being an American citizen. Some countries have very few, if any, freedoms.

Some people define freedom as the willingness to do any and every immoral action out there with no reserve or moral compass that it might be wrong. Many think freedom means they can choose whatever they want to do. One might call this moral relativism, meaning if it feels good to you then you have the freedom to do it, with no repercussions.

For those who claim Christ as Lord and Saviour, His blood has set them free from death, sin, hell, the grave, and the bondage of sin. We don't stand condemned because of our sin, but we stand in His love and freedom. Being free means we are not in bondage to sin. When you have freedom, you do not isolate yourself, but you give of yourself to others, and to God.

Yes, God has given us freedom. He has redeemed us with His blood. His grace and mercies are new every morning. His grace covers His children, and His love has made our salvation possible. However, to live a victorious Christian life, you and I cannot use that grace as an opportunity to continue sinning and living life any way we choose. There must be a difference in how we live, and how the world lives.

Jesus said, "Be holy, for I am holy." Romans 6:1, 2 tells us that it is completely unacceptable to continue in a pattern of sin while using grace as a way to excuse it. We bring ourselves out of the blessings of God and invite God's discipline when we willingly toy around with sin. If we died with Christ to sin, then we cannot willingly drink the poison of sin and get away with it. This doesn't mean we must be perfect, but there must be a continual thirst and chasing after the holiness of Christ.

True freedom means you worship God in spirit and in truth. John 4:24 tells us that "those who worship God must worship Him in Spirit and in truth." When we worship, it should not be out of religious obligation, but out of a hunger for God and a Spirit-led love for Him. The Spirit of God in the Bible is referred to as the *Pneuma*, or the breath of God or wind from Heaven. There is also the river of God's love as we read about in Revelation and Ezekiel, which flows down from the throne of Heaven. We each have the opportunity to jump into the river when we worship and feel the presence of the Spirit of God.

Challenge (Action Step):

Think of all Jesus has done in your life. Think of how and write down the bondage of sin He delivered you from. Write down all the ways you may have used to be in bondage prior to Christ, and thank God for His freedom. Do you worship God in Spirit and truth in His freedom, or do you barely give Him anything at all when you worship

Him? Think of the freedom that has come to your life? Do you serve God with joy and thanksgiving in your heart or is it from a place of religious duty. Maybe you need to re-align some of your priorities to make God as your center and chief aim in life.

Meditate at least 15 minutes a day on Galatians 5:1. It is for freedom that Christ has set you free, stand firm then and do not let yourself be burdened again to a yoke of slavery.

A yoke is something that controls an ox from the time it is very young, and the ox will grow into it as it grows and fully matures. In the same way, yokes can be put unto us when we are very young. There may be verbal, physical, sexual, or emotional abuse that young children face. It doesn't have to be that severe.

A yoke can be the anger in your heart that you have each and every day when you observe your father correcting or criticizing your mom or maybe walking by you without giving you a hug or telling you he loved you. This yoke of anger will grow into bitterness and hatred for your father. One day, this yoke will control you to the point that you do the very same thing to your wife or children.

A yoke can be the feeling of being unloved because your father left early every morning to go to work before you woke up, not having a warm, affectionate hug from him or maybe being physically or emotionally absent in your home. You could also have a yoke because your parents divorced when you were young, and you are filled with hurt and unforgiveness towards them for that, and maybe you promised yourself or out of anger you vowed you would never put your children through the same type of hurt.

Yet now, because of the law of judgments in Matthew 7, you find yourself in a marriage you cannot stand, contemplating divorce. To lay aside this yoke, you must begin the process of forgiving the parents from whom you received the hurt. Renounce vows in Jesus' name and replace any lies you may be believing about yourself and replace them with the truth of God's Word. Recognize any judgments you may have made towards your parents, siblings, and repent of them.

Ask the Lord Jesus to flood your heart with His love and cleanse you of any defilement, pain, wounds, or lies. Ask the Holy Spirit to show you any more unhealed areas of your heart and help you to walk into a new way of holiness.

Consider repeating this process of prayer, choosing to forgive, and cleansing by the Holy Spirit and personal reflection every day until you believe that you are free.

JOURNAL NOTES

DAY 25 – REPENT

Matthew 4:17
From that time Jesus began to preach and to say, 'Repent, for the kingdom of heaven is at hand.'

RIGHT AFTER JESUS WAS first baptized and then affirmed by His Heavenly Father, He was driven into the wilderness by the Holy Spirit, where He fasted 40 days in the desert. He defeated Satan with the power of the spoken Word of God and proved Himself to be victorious over the temptations of Satan. After this He began His ministry.

Jesus' first message was, "Repent for the Kingdom of Heaven is at hand." It's interesting to note that Jesus' first message was to repent for the Kingdom of Heaven was at hand. The Word for Kingdom is *Basileia,* meaning the dominion, rule, reign, the exercise of kingly power, or the spiritual kingdom, domain, or the glorious reign of the Messiah. Jesus was saying that the rule and reign of Christ had come or it was at hand, ready to grasp. But first the people had to repent (*metanoia*) or change their mindset or way of thinking. Jesus had come, who would end the OT law and usher in a new law of His Holy Spirit. If the Jewish people of Israel were going to access the Kingdom of God through Jesus, they would need to change the ways they had been thinking.

The same is true for us. If we are going to live in the Kingdom of God on earth, we must change our ways of thinking and completely put an end to some sinful, childish ways. Living in the Kingdom of Heaven requires dwelling with Jesus in Heavenly places by how we think and act, and not allowing the Kingdom of this world to influence our behaviors, thoughts, and actions. We cannot live in two kingdoms at the same time. We must solely live our lives controlled by the Kingdom of Heaven.

When we look at the Apostle Paul, we see a picture of someone who truly repented and changed his entire way of living. He was heading to persecute Christians and have them martyred, and Jesus intercepted His plans and caused Him to completely change His way of thinking from a persecutor to a radical Christ follower and missionary evangelist. He didn't excuse His behavior, but He immediately stopped what he was doing, repented, and changed the way He was going, and followed Jesus. The light of Christ that shone on Him was so powerful that it blinded him and immediately he heard the voice of Jesus who he had been persecuting. After Paul saw the light of Christ and heard His voice, he changed course. Out of obedience, Paul repented and God used Him mightily to spread the gospel to the known world.

One reason so many people are so slow to repent is that both in America and throughout the world, both in and out of the body of Christ, there is no longer a fear of God. There is no longer a reverence and respect for Him. People enjoy staying stuck in their sin and brokenness. So many become comfortable in their sin and bondage, and there is no consciousness or conviction of sin. Once this happens there may not be a conviction by the Holy Spirit to change. As a general rule, I do believe the vast majority in the body of Christ have lost their fear or respect for God. Turn on the news today, and we can see that the world, and of course America, is filled with darkness. It is obvious that the nations of this world have lost touch with God or any sort of morality. There must be an awakening and returning to our first love for Jesus in America and the nations of the earth!

God is a good, perfect loving Heavenly Father, He is wanting to welcome with open arms, any who will come to Him. Romans 8:37-39 tells us that we cannot measure the amount of love that God has for us. We cannot measure the height, depth, length, or width, or breadth of the love that God has for us. In fact, as these verses tell us, that God wants to do an exceeding abundance in our lives, "above all that we can think of or imagine."

Romans 8:37-39 tells us that nothing on earth or in heaven can separate us from the love of God. "For I am persuaded that neither death nor life, nor angels nor principalities nor powers, nor things present nor things to come, nor height nor depth, nor any other created thing, shall be able to separate us from the love of God which is in Christ Jesus our Lord."

Yes, there is a lack of the fear of God in our society today, but it is so rewarding to come to Christ. His love is limitless and indescribable. If you are struggling with a sin please know that it is never too late to come to God in repentance. Romans 2:4 tells us that it is the goodness of God which leads to repentance. I implore you to understand how vast God's love for you is. He wants you to receive His love, but sin will block us from truly receiving and feeling God's love and hearing His voice. You should daily be examining your heart and identifying any areas for which you should be repenting. This is why Paul tells us to work out our salvation with fear and trembling.

Challenge (Action Step):

Daily read the Word of God and meditate on what the Holy Spirit might have you repent of.

Is there any known, blatant sin in your life you know is repulsive or dishonoring to God?

Meditate on the wonder of God's infinite love for you. Focus on how God has showered you with His love. Read Ephesians 3:14-21 and Psalm 139:17-18 and consider how amazing God's love for you is. Consider the fullness of God's love and how we cannot understand the height, depth, or width, or length of His love. In fact, to understand His love is beyond our understanding! Meditate on how much God loves you. Ask for his love to fill your heart and wash away all hurt and defilement.

JOURNAL NOTES

SECTION SIX: WILL OF GOD

DAY 26 – GO MAKE DISCIPLES!

Matthew 28:18-20

And Jesus came and spoke to them, saying, 'All authority has been given to Me in heaven and on earth. 19 Go therefore and make disciples of all the nations, baptizing them in the name of the Father and of the Son and of the Holy Spirit, 20 teaching them to observe all things that I have commanded you; and lo, I am with you always, even to the end of the age.' Amen.

Acts 1:8

But you shall receive power when the Holy Spirit has come upon you; and you shall be witnesses to Me in Jerusalem, and in all Judea and Samaria, and to the end of the earth.

Mark 16:15
And He said to them, 'Go into all the world and preach the gospel to every creature.'

G OD SAVES HIS CHILDREN to not just get a free ticket to Heaven. We are saved and called with a mission to fulfill. We are called to make disciples, but also to build His Kingdom on the earth. We are to be a "witness" or a living testament of God's love to others. Everywhere you and I touch should be impacted by our witness and by the love of Christ. If we are truly carrying the love of Christ to a lost and dying world, everything you and I touch should be positively impacted. We should be leaving our mark in every place we go. To make a disciple everywhere you go, means you should be leaving people with a desire to become disciples of Jesus Christ. You, as the salt of the earth, should leave a taste in peoples' mouths, which makes them want the Jesus you have. Your life should exude excellence.

Your life should portray the glory of God that will cause people to want the Jesus you have, because of your testimony. People should be changed, environments should be changed, and institutions or establishments should be benefited and improved just by the merit of you being there. Acts 1:8 tells us that the disciples would receive power once the Holy Spirit had come upon them. "But you shall receive power when the Holy Spirit has come upon you; and you shall be witnesses to Me in

Jerusalem, and in all Judea and Samaria, and to the end of the earth."

The same principle applies to Christians today. We only operate with our own power before the Holy Spirit comes upon us. When we receive the Holy Spirit, everything changes. The Holy Spirit is who enables the Christian to walk in power, anointing, and greatness. After Jesus ascended to Heaven, the disciples prayed and fasted for 50 days before the Holy Spirit came at Pentecost. Prayer is the key to ushering in the presence of the Holy Spirit upon one's life. Oral Roberts would pray alone for at least an hour before each service or crusade he conducted.

Jesus tells us in Matthew 28 to go and make disciples of all nations. Yes, this can involve preaching, but the main way Jesus wants His children to make disciples is by first loving them. We could say, "Go into all the world and make disciples by loving people where they are at." Matthew 25:40 tells us that when we act by being the hands and feet of Christ to the world (the least of these), we are also ministering to Him.

Making disciples is not just preaching to people until you are blue in the face. Making disciples is first converting people, but then making them into followers of Christ. Making disciples can be an ongoing process of discipling and pouring into someone and helping to make them into a faithful, devoted Christ follower. Our job is to cast the net and plant the seeds and the Holy Spirit will do the work of convicting and bringing in the harvest.

God has called us to share in the message of salvation through Christ to not just our family and friends and people we are comfortable with, but also with those who might not be particularly like us. We are to share the love of Christ with the least of these and with those society might reject. For you, this might be those in the LGBT community or someone in poverty, or from a particular cultural or racial background you are not particularly familiar or comfortable with. Jesus hung out with those whom the society of His day labeled as outcasts and rejects. He simply loved them. He didn't support the bad choices they may have been making or condone the sinful lifestyles they may have been participating in. In fact, he called them to a different lifestyle, which was one of holiness and Christlikeness.

One way we make disciples, besides preaching the Gospel and showing people our love is by simply excelling in the tasks God has put before us on the earth. There is something called excellence, and when you live your life with excellence, the world will notice.

Paul tells us in Colossians 3:23 Amp, "Whatever you do [whatever your task may be], work from the soul [that is, put in your very best effort], as [something done] for the Lord and not for men." When we work as unto the Lord in everything we do, then God is glorified and the world will take notice. Excellence will always be a witness to others. God has already laid out ahead of time the people you will encounter, and He has laid out and orchestrated the good works you will need and have to be a blessing to others.

Ephesians 2:10 tells us, "And he laid out the good works ahead of time so that we should walk in them." God has already lined people up in your path for you to show the love of Christ to. You never know the power of a personal witness.

Challenge (Action Step):

Start with your family, your friends, your school, your class, your job and begin with practical steps by planting seeds of love and kindness. Be thoughtful. Ask how their day is going. Pat them on the shoulder to tell them you care about them. Offer to give them a glass of water, buy a meal for them, or invite them for coffee or over for dinner. Then start asking them questions. You can tell them your own personal testimony of something God has done in your own life.

The Bible tells us we overcome by the blood of the Lamb and the Word of our testimony. The Gospel is simple. Romans 10:9 tells us, "that if you confess with your mouth the Lord Jesus and believe in your heart that God has raised Him from the dead, you will be saved." Simply believe in the Lord Jesus Christ and that God rose Him from the grave, and you will be saved. Believe in Christ and you will be saved from your sin. It's important to believe, but there must be a heart change.

Your heart must change from longing for things of this world to longing for things of Christ. There must be the 12-inch drop from you head knowledge to your heart. The love of God must flood your heart. This may not happen on day one. It's a continual process of thirsting after righteousness and chasing after God. You must explain this to them. After their initial conversion experience, they must continue to grow in their salvation. They must get into community with other believers. A Bible believing church would be the best way to make this happen. They should continue studying the Word of God.

After Paul's conversion, he spent three years in Arabia, probably a desert area, studying and meditating on the Word of God. He also conferred with some of the apostles and key disciples about His conversion. New believers need to have regular Bible study and need someone teaching them the basic truths of scripture. You should explain to them the importance of living a lifestyle of repentance.

JOURNAL NOTES

DAY 27 – UNITY IN CHRIST

Philippians 2:2-4
2 fulfill my joy by being like-minded, having the same love, being of one accord, of one mind. 3 Let nothing be done through selfish ambition or conceit, but in lowliness of mind let each esteem others better than himself. 4 Let each of you look out not only for his own interests, but also for the interests of others.

Galatians 3:28
There is neither Jew nor Greek, there is neither slave nor free, there is neither male nor female; for you are all one in Christ Jesus.

Colossians 3:14
But above all these things put on love, which is the bond of perfection.

1 Corinthians 1:10
Now I plead with you, brethren, by the name of our Lord Jesus Christ, that you all speak the same thing, and that there be no divisions among you, but that you be perfectly joined together in the same mind and in the same judgment.

John 17:20-22
20 I do not pray for these alone, but also for those who will believe in Me through their word; 21 that they all may be one, as You, Father, are in Me, and I in You; that they also may be one in Us, that the world may believe that You sent Me. 22 And the glory which You gave Me I have given them, that they may be one just as We are one:

John 3:16
For God so loved the world that He gave His only begotten Son, that whoever believes in Him should not perish but have everlasting life.

I N OUR WORLD TODAY, we see society and culture plagued with disagreements, hate, division, and divisiveness. People are looking for reasons to become angry and riot or fight with others. Turn on the news at any time, and you will see countless stories of conflict, hate, and unrest, not just in America, but all over the world.

The Bible has told us that all these things will happen. Things are not going to get any better before the end of time when Jesus returns. This just provides the believers with opportunities to shine the light and love of Christ into different broken situations and hurting people.

As Philippians 2 tells us, we should seek to be of the same mind and being in one accord with people of faith. We must stop looking for reasons to be upset with others in our churches.

Philippians 2:3 highlights it well for us. Paul tells us, "Let nothing be done through selfish ambition or conceit, but in lowliness of mind let each esteem others better than Himself." Everything we do in life should be done from the place of humility and selflessness. We must lay down our egos and wanting to be right about everything. We must understand that God has placed us on the earth on assignment, to spread the love of Christ to those God has put in our path. In fact, this is part of making Disciples.

God instructed us to walk in love towards all men, meaning those around us (Ephesians 5:1,2). This does not mean we may necessarily have to agree with all men, but we should have a love and compassion for people. God desires us to be in unity with all those in the body of Christ, even ones we may not necessarily agree with on every point, and to walk with Christ-like love, grace, and compassion towards those outside the body of Christ.

I like how Philippians 2:4 talks about it. We should not just look out for our own interests, but also for the interests of others. This is a Christ-like servant's mindset. Philippians 2:2 compels us to be "like-minded and to be of one accord." We must not align ourselves with all the wickedness, cultural practices, and ways of this world, but we can be "like-minded and of one accord with those inside the body of Christ. We should strive to be lights in the darkness by always looking for ways to serve those around us, whether they be in the world or outside the world. The Bible says to be in the world but not of the world.

In John 17:21 Jesus prays that His followers would all be one (in unity) as they are one in the Father (God). When the world sees the children of God being in unity with each other, because they are in unity with God the Father, then the world will want the Jesus that we have. If the body of Christ could truly get along, learn to forgive and love each other, then we would truly see the world changed.

As believers in Christ, we should all have a mission and focus. Our main objective should be making disciples and changing the world for Christ. The more you and I learn to live in unity with those around us in the body of Christ, live selfless, Christ-like lives, the more productive and fruitful we will be in fulfilling the mission God has placed us on the earth to accomplish, which is to build His Kingdom and make disciples or followers of Christ.

Colossians 3:14 sums it up pretty well for us. Paul says in this verse, "Above all things, put on love, which is the bond of perfection." The word for love here is agape love. This is the type of love God has for us. He never stops loving us. Agape love is choosing to love without expecting anything in return. The word for perfection is *teleiotes.* It means the state of completeness or mental or moral perfection. God wants us to walk in Christ-filled, perfect love towards our family, friends, and outsiders, and not expect to receive anything back from them. This can only happen when we have a heart of purity, devoid of unforgiveness, anger, or bitterness. When we walk in agape love towards others, then this will create a sense of harmony and completeness in each of those relationships we encounter.

John 3:16 tells us that God so loved the world that He gave his only begotten Son that whoever believes in Him shall not perish but have eternal life."

What does this tell us? God gave His most prized possession for the world's Salvation, knowing Jesus would be mocked, spit upon, beaten beyond human recognition, and nailed to a cross to die a humiliating death. God still sent His Son, Jesus, knowing He would die this way, and He still loves and forgives all who come to Him in faith and belief in His Son Jesus and in His death on the cross.

This is the type of love we must have. We must choose to love our family, friends, co-workers, employers, employees, customers, and the world around us with this type of love. We should choose to love the ones around us and seek to be in unity even if those we are loving may turn against us or hurt us. God loved the world, but He does not allow the ones in sin to stay stuck in their sin if they want a relationship with Him. Those who want to be in fellowship with Him must repent of sin and live a lifestyle of repentance, chasing after holiness.

Jesus loves you and He died for you, but He doesn't want you to stay stuck in your bondage. He died so you might live an abundant life of freedom, not living in the consequences of sin and bondage. This is the love with which you are called to love others. This is how you can live in unity with those you once thought you would be unable to live with or associate with. Lay down your pride. Lay down your life.

Challenge (Action Step):

How do you need to change your thoughts or ways of thinking so that you walk in love towards those in your family, workplace, or even the world?

What bitterness or prejudices do you need to repent for?

Is there any resentment you need to repent for?

What is keeping you from living in unity with your family or church members? How do you need to change your thought processes or what sinful behaviors do you need to repent for?

Ask for the love of God to flood your heart and heal you of all defilement or bitterness, and unforgiveness.

Ask for Jesus to show you any and every sin or bitterness, unforgiveness, or even judgment that may be keeping you stuck in isolation, bitterness, or isolation.

Ask God to show you any pride you may have and repent. Ask for Christ to give you the ability to live with humility. Look for ways to live with humility and a servant's heart. Seek to be in unity with others.

Ask God for the ability to be able to walk in the fullness of God's love each and every day.

Read and meditate on Ephesians 3:14-27.

JOURNAL NOTES

Day 28 – Walk by Faith And Not by Sight

Hebrews 4:12
For the word of God is living and powerful, and sharper than any two-edged sword, piercing even to the division of soul and spirit, and of joints and marrow, and is a discerner of the thoughts and intents of the heart.

John 6:63
It is the Spirit who gives life; the flesh profits nothing. The words that I speak to you are spirit, and they are life.

L AST NIGHT I WENT to pray for a man in a coma in the ICU. From all appearances, it appeared that he was completely unresponsive. I know this man's story. Many, including myself, have been praying constantly for him since he had his brain injury and experienced some damage to his brain stem. At first, the doctors wanted to pull the plugs, take him off life support, and give his organs to someone else. However, his wife refused, for she was convinced that he was not dead, but his spirit was very much alive.

It is a miracle of God that he is still alive. I applaud his wife's strong will and faith not to give in to the doctor's wishes. Their story reminds me of my own story of survival and my parents, notably my mom, fighting for my life when all those in the hospital tried to convince her to take me off life support.

The word of God is alive and powerful and sharper than any two-edged sword, piercing even to the division of soul and spirit, of joints and marrow, and is a discerner of the thoughts and intentions of the heart (Hebrews 4:12). Jesus said, "My words are spirit, and they are life." (John 6:63) As I stood there looking at the man in a coma, I didn't see his present condition. I saw him as the pastor God had called him to be. I began to read the word over him and pray over him. God responds to faith. I could have been content to sit at my house and pray, but out of faith and obedience to the spirit of God, I went to visit him and pray with him and his family in the hospital.

God calls us not to be content to sit in our homes or comfort zones, pray, or do works for God. God calls his children to take bold steps of faith and obedience to his voice. God has called you to get out of your comfort zone and go be the hands and feet of Christ and serve others. God has called you and I to go forward and bear fruit that will lead to change and breakthrough for people.

In whatever situation you find yourself, or that God may be leading you to pray for or involve yourself in, God wants us to make bold steps for him. I stood there praying for the man in the coma. I did not see him in the coma, but I saw him as the preacher he was. The verse came to me, "How beautiful are the feet of those who bring good news to the poor."

It also reminded me that when God redeems us in our lost or broken condition, he already sees our true potential. He sees our whole redeemed self. He doesn't know the brokenness we carry or the baggage which is way down. God sees the man or woman of God we will become. So God redeems us and grants salvation to us because he loves us unconditionally, and he sees the person we will become because of his son, Jesus, operating and living through us.

God saw, and I had an idea of what the man in the coma would become but it will take a lot of work and rehabilitation to become the man God had called him to be. God already sees the man or woman you will become, but it will take some work (discipline, laying aside the weights) to get you there. Holiness and our purpose do not get served to us on a platter. There is work to get there.

God responds to our faith and obedience. How much trust and obedience are you willing to walk in? Are you ready to lay down your life? I challenge you to lay your life down for Christ and walk into his glory and anointing. It is by faith!

Challenge (Action Step):

Have you been walking by faith and not by sight? Have you actively put your trust in Jesus and in his words in the Bible and if so, how? How often do you spend building your faith each day? Your faith is like a muscle, and the more you exercise it and use it, the stronger your faith in God will grow and the more power from God you will receive.

2 Timothy 1:7 tells us, "For God has not given us a spirit of fear, but of power, love, and a sound mind." Begin walking by faith, in love for God, and He will embolden you with a spirit of power and sound mind in your decisions and life today!

Begin today doing the necessary work to begin a lifestyle of holiness. Begin reading the Word of God. Begin worshiping and praying to God. Begin asking God to show you areas in your life you need to change. What weights do you need to lay aside which might be keeping you from fixing your eyes on Jesus, the author and finisher of your faith?

(Consider Hebrews 12:1, 2) "Therefore we also, since we are surrounded by so great a cloud of witnesses, let us lay aside every weight, and the sin which so easily ensnares *us*, and let us run with endurance the race that is set before us,

2 looking unto Jesus, the author and finisher of *our* faith, who for the joy that was set before Him endured the cross, despising the shame, and has sat down at the right hand of the throne of God."

JOURNAL NOTES

DAY 29 – WORSHIPING GOD AND LOVING PEOPLE

Galatians 5:14
For all the law is fulfilled in one word, even in this: 'You shall love your neighbor as yourself.'

Matthew 22:36-40
'Teacher, which is the great commandment in the law?' Jesus said to him, "'You shall love the Lord your God with all your heart, with all your soul, and with all your mind.' This is the first and great commandment. And the second is like it: 'You shall love your neighbor as yourself.' On these two commandments hang all the Law and the Prophets."

J ESUS TOLD US THE greatest commandments were to love God with all our hearts, with all our souls, and with all our minds. And to love our neighbor or fellow man, as ourselves.

Think about it. If you are truly loving God with ALL your heart, soul, and mind, than your thoughts, intentions, and actions are controlled by Him. If everything about our lives flows from a place of infinite love for God, then loving our neighbor will come naturally. If your heart has been filled with the fullness of God's love then everything in your life will fall into place in alignment with God's will.

Out of a love for God, your life will flow and produce love for others. God wants us to walk in the agape love towards others. It means pure, willful, sacrificial love where we desire the highest good for the other person. It is love that expects nothing in return. This is the type of love God wants us to give to others. We are to love others the same way Christ loved us. He willingly gave Himself for us so that we might receive salvation, when we did not deserve it. The way we have this love in our hearts for others is by first having a heart of purity and allowing the love of God to flood our hearts each and every day. Ask God to give you this love in your heart. Read and meditate on the love of God and ask Christ to flood your mind and cleanse your heart and mind of all defilement.

Love is not a suggestion, but it is a command actually. Galatians 5:14 tells us that the whole law is fulfilled in one word, which is to love our neighbor as ourselves. Once we love God with all our heart, soul, mind, and strength, everything will flow from this place of love. The only way to truly love God is to love Him from a heart of purity, free from sin and defilement. One of the keys is to make sure your heart is in the right place. Make sure your heart is free of any defilement, pain, or resentment. Make sure your motives are right. Does your heart burn for Jesus, above all other desires?

When we love God and act out of that love toward others by serving them, this will create not only joy in our lives, but also a renewed sense of hope and joy. Serving creates a positive mindset. Serving creates energy and joy in our lives, because we are being the hands and feet of Christ. Through service, you are doing what God has placed you on this earth to do, which is to walk in the good works He has placed in front of you (Ephesians 2:10) by loving and serving those in need.

Challenge (Action Step):

Our lives should be worship to our Creator. By serving others, we worship God. By doing everything we do in life, as unto the Lord, we worship God. By forgiving, serving, meeting needs, loving others, reconciling with our neighbors, and by planting seeds of kindness, and by showing others how much we love and care for them, we worship God.

So your entire life can be one big act of worship to Him, when you do the mission He has called you to do in life. What does the Bible say, "Those who worship Him must worship Him in Spirit and in truth." This is how you should live your life. You should live by the power of the Holy Spirit, and by living in truth, being the truth of God's Word, and in holiness. Everything you do in life can be turned into worship to God simply by your living by the Holy Spirit and by the truth of God's Word. Evaluate your life and determine if your motives and actions are focused on building your kingdom or His kingdom.

A life lived solely for oneself is self-worship, and dishonoring and loathsome to God. I challenge you to live your life in worship only to Jesus. Examine your life and determine what needs to change. Choose to forgive as Christ forgave you; choose to work as unto the Lord; choose to play out of the joy of knowing God; choose to reconcile because God has reconciled you to Himself; choose to act out of worship and love for God, because He is worthy; choose to think with the mind of Christ, choose to serve because Christ came to this earth to serve you and I, and choose to live in holiness out of love and worship for Jesus, who alone is worthy.

JOURNAL NOTES

Day 30 – Occupy Until He Comes

Read Luke 19:11-27

Romans 13:11
And do this, knowing the time, that now it is high time to awake out of sleep; for now our salvation is nearer than when we first believed.

Matthew 24:10-14
And then many will be offended, will betray one another, and will hate one another. Then many false prophets will rise up and deceive many. And because lawlessness will abound,

the love of many will grow cold. But he who
endures to the end shall be saved. And this
gospel of the kingdom will be preached in all
the world as a witness to all the nations, and
then the end will come.

M ANY OF YOU HAVE probably heard someone say the phrase, "We've got to occupy till He comes." This is actually taken from the passage in Luke 19:11-27 where Jesus gives the parable about the minas and how the master of a certain estate goes on a trip and leaves his servants with each a certain number of minas, which was a form of currency in Jesus' time.

One servant invested it, and it earned 10 minas. Another servant invested the money, and it earned 5 minas. To both of these servants, the master of the estate said, "Well done, good and faithful servant." These servants represent God's children who wisely invest what God has given to them. They reap a reward for their rewards and inherit a prize in the Kingdom of God. When Jesus comes back at the end of the age, He will say, "Well done, my good and faithful servants."

The other servant took the minas or talent that the master of the house gave him, and hid it in a handkerchief, and could only give the mina back when the master of the house returned. This represents the person who does nothing with the life God gives him. When he stands before the judgment seat, he will have nothing to show for the life he lived, and unfortunately God will say, "Depart from me, you worker of iniquity, I never knew you." God gives each of us the breath in our lungs. However, it is up to us as to how we will use the life with which He has entrusted us. Will you live your life for Jesus and receive an eternal reward, or will you live your life for yourself and receive back nothing but condemnation?

This is why the master of the house tells the servants to "Do business or occupy till I come." These are the same words of Christ to come. Don't get caught up with the fear and chaos of everything going on in the world. We need to be busy about the Father's business until Jesus returns and be found faithful when He comes back. God has given you talents, gifts, and abilities to use for his glory to impact this world for Christ.

The return of Christ Is imminent, and we can all agree that things are going crazy all over the world. Wars are erupting worldwide, and the threat of war is increasing. The world is plagued by plagues and we each have the opportunity to give into fear over everything happening in the world. The commands of Christ to us are simple: "Occupy till he comes." We must not change our commitment to Christ during these troublesome times.

We must not allow fear to control us and ruin our commitment to Christ. Jesus promised us that those who overcome these last days will receive the crown of life. In these challenging times we are living in, God does not want our love for Jesus to grow cold, but to grow hotter and hotter and more and more on fire, as we see the day of Christ approaching. The temptation today is to cower away in fear, give up, and give into the lawlessness that is abounding in this world.

What does it look like to be "he or she who overcomes?" It means you don't give into fear over everything falling apart. You don't allow fear to control you, but you allow Jesus to control you. This means your heart must be filled with the fullness of His love. This means that you don't stay angry or offended, but you choose to forgive continually. This means you don't give into the sway of the sinful ways and practices of this world. Simply put, the phrase, "one who overcomes" is one who endures, keeping their eyes on Jesus, the author and finisher of their faith, as we read in Hebrews 12:1-2.

The "one who overcomes" is one who refuses to give up. The "one who overcomes" is the one who continues showing up, continues putting in the effort, continues loving, and continues forgiving. You keep your eyes on Jesus so that no matter what happens, you are daily looking to Jesus by seeking Him and trusting Him fully. You aren't looking at this world as it is falling apart, but you are shifting your focus to Jesus by meditating on His Word no matter what.

You can't isolate yourself, but you must seek Christian fellowship with others in the Body of Christ. Daily, each morning, immerse yourself in the love of God by reading and meditating on the Word of God. Allow His love to permeate your heart and ask the Holy Spirit to heal you of all wounds, hurts, and pain. There is a race for you to run. There is a prize for you to win. You must not let the chaos of this life cause you to miss out on the best that God has for you. Choose a lifestyle of forgiveness. Choose a lifestyle of holiness. Choose a lifestyle of fixing your eyes on Jesus and saying no to fear but saying yes to Jesus. Luke 21 tells us that men's hearts will fail them for fear. Do not let your heart fail because of fear of everything going on, but earnestly seek to become unshakeable in the love of God.

Challenge (Action Step):

Hebrews 12:1, 2 "Therefore we also, since we are surrounded by so great a cloud of witnesses, let us lay aside every weight, and the sin which so easily ensnares *us*, and let us run with endurance the race that is set before us, 2 looking unto Jesus, the author and finisher of *our* faith, who for the joy that was set before Him endured the cross, despising the shame, and has sat down at the right hand of the throne of God."

Strive for the next three weeks to daily get into the Word of God in the mornings or sometime and study His Word, and put that Word into action by putting yourself into those situations. Twenty-one days is the time that it takes to establish new patterns or habits. Don't stop at 21 days, but continue the habit of beginning each day with Bible study and by asking the Holy Spirit to speak to you. Ask God to show you any sins or weights you need to repent of or let go of. Examine your heart and ask God to show you any ounce of unforgiveness or bitterness.

Ask God to show you a positive, uplifting community you can join either in your church or somewhere close where you can plug into healthy, encouraging Christian fellowship.

Daily pray to God and ask Him to give you the strength to look unto Jesus the entire day and resist sin in all of its manifestations. Seek reconciliation in all your relationships where there may be hostility or brokenness.

Daily read Ephesians 3:14-21 and ask God to fill you with the fullness of His love.

Recognize any lies of the enemy you are living under. John 8:44 tells us that Satan is the father of lies. Repent for any ways you are or have been listening to the lies of the enemy. Sometimes we listen to the lies of the enemy about ourselves, our family, our co-workers, our friends, everything and it can cause us to do and say things which can bring devastation and heartache to others, all because of a lie we believed. God's Word is truth, and He wants us to live in truth. God does not want us to live under the lies of the enemy but in the truth of God's Word and only listening to His voice and worshiping Him.

For every lie you believe, replace it with the truth of God's Word and practice renouncing every lie and come out of agreement with the enemy. Allow the truth of God's Word to flood your heart and ask for His Word to replace all the lies. It will take time, but you can replace all lies with God's truth. You must repent of all bitterness and unforgiveness. Daily you must be awakened to God's love.

Once you are in this lifestyle of daily being awakened to God's love, and burning in your love for Him, God wants you to share that love with others. God wants you to build His Kingdom by sharing the light and love of Christ with those you come into contact with. Look for ways by looking for practical ways to show the love of God to others. Choose to love; choose to serve; choose to forgive.

JOURNAL NOTES

ABOUT THE AUTHOR

WILL BOGGS IV IS a minister of the Gospel. He has been passion-driven by compassion to awaken a generation from the spiritual slumber and coma many find themselves in. He has been married to Mariah Boggs since May 2016, and has two beautiful daughters, Elizabeth and Elianna, along with a baby boy, William Levi.

Will and Mariah met at Liberty University. Mariah served with her family as missionaries to South Africa with the IMB for 8 years. Will has a bachelor's degree in pastoral leadership from Liberty University. He has studied at Asbury and Fuller Theological Seminaries. He has a leadership position at Living Waters Ministry and has founded the Awaken Movement. Newly, he joined Matthews 10 Ministries, with Dr. Pete Sulack, as an associate evangelist.

SOURCES

This book was comprised from multiple sources.

- http://gcfrog.com/publishing/wp-content/uploads/2016/05/Standard%20Page%20Order%20Of%20A%20Book.pdf

- https://www.intandemdigitalpress.com/post/standard-order-of-sections-in-a-book

- https://www.authorlearningcenter.com/publishing/design/w/interior/7084/interior-parts-of-a-book-front-matter-text-and-back-matter

- https://scribemedia.com/parts-of-book/#:~:text=Series%20Title%20Page,by%20%5BYour%20Name%5D%E2%80%A6%E2%80%9D

CONNECT WITH US!

www.theawakenmovement.com

@willboggsiv

@willboggs2

@awakeageneration

@Awakenwill777

@Awakenmovement7

Matthew 10 International
Matthew10.com/will